MIRACLE MILES
For God's Special People

Dear Marlys,

I Pray the stories of our travels
for Shepherds, will be a blessing.
Thanks for your friendship.

Ralph J. Poulson

(Philip 1:20)   P.O. Box 1884
                Ferndale 98248

MIRACLE MILES

For God's Special People

Stories gleaned while traveling for Shepherds Ministries,
whose main goal was helping individuals with
developmental disabilities

RALPH J. POULSON

XULON PRESS

Xulon Press
2301 Lucien Way #415
Maitland, FL 32751
407.339.4217
www.xulonpress.com

Printed in the United States of America.

ISBN-13: 9781545651018

MIRACLE MILES

For God's special people

INTRODUCTION

Traveling for Shepherds, a unique Christian home and school for individuals with intellectual disabilities, was something we never thought of during the years our daughter Joy lived there. We visited Shepherds each furlough from Brazil, and as often as we could while pastoring in Washington State. After a blessed eighteen years as pastor of First Baptist Church in Ferndale, Washington, the position of west coast representative for Shepherds opened to us.

Shepherds is well known by many in this country. We did not desire, nor were we prepared to write a history of this wonderful place. After getting into the routine of our new ministry as representative, we were challenged about what we were doing.

The Shepherds residents were the reason we visited churches soliciting prayer and financial support. The purpose of these chapters is not to give personal biographies of those to whom Shepherds ministered. Occasionally allusions are made to some of the poignant happenings at Shepherds, without mentioning names. The only exception to this self-imposed rule, is our daughter Joy.

As we traveled, a pattern was forming that impressed us. Coupled with the delights of presenting Shepherds to churches, were the amazing added blessings that happened daily. This book shares some of those intriguing stories. We hope you will relate to some, and rejoice with us for the delightful way God blessed us in this ministry. I enjoyed placing Bible verses at the end of each story. Many have expressed their thanks for this.

MARGIE POULSON (July 16, 1930--October 19, 2017)

I was not expecting to write these final words. My dear wife, Margie, had a stroke October 10, 2017, just as I was going out the door for my weekly volunteer day at our church as an elder. That day, my life changed. Before I left, she spoke to me, but her words were terribly garbled. I called 911, and she left our home for the last time. After ten days of loving care, but much suffering, at St. Joseph Hospital in Bellingham, WA., she died at 10:15 pm October 19, 2017. At last she was safe in the arms of Jesus. My son Rawlie was with me at home when I received the call at 10:30 pm, and we went to the hospital to gather her things. The memorial service was October

29, 2017, in our church, First Baptist of Ferndale, WA. It was the largest attendance I had ever seen in the sixty-five years I have been a member there.

Life is not the same now. Everything reminds me of her, and that is good. She is the one who did all the research for this book, extracting ideas from our journals, and I wrote the stories. I wanted so much for her to see the finished product, but after all, she read all of it before it even went to the editor. So even though this book is dedicated to our dear friends at Shepherds, in my heart Margie is at the heart of this book. Her love for Shepherds had no limits. Every mile driven those eleven years meant so much to her. Every church meeting was another opportunity to tell people about Shepherds as she stood at the literature table before and after each meeting. Her declining health, and my age, and Shepherds, dictated to our hearts that it was time to terminate this ministry. I am thrilled to think of the communion Margie must be having with our daughter Joy, who in this life never spoke a word. To God be the glory.

DEDICATION

To Tracy Terrill, President
Dr. William J. Amstutz, Chancellor
Daniel DiDonato, former Vice-President of Development
Brian Page, Vice-President of Advancement
To all members of the Boards
All staff persons
All who are serving or have served at Shepherds

To Joy A. Poulson (daughter)
(October 31, 1959—July 21,2012)
Marjorie A. Poulson (wife)
July 16, 1930—October 19, 2017

Ernest N. Poulson
April 1, 1995—October 13, 2017

Harold E. Poulson
(Who funded the printing of this book)

I HUMBLY DEDICATE THIS BOOK.

To each of you, and many whose names do not appear
here, we are sincerely grateful. Your individual and collec-
tive efforts have produced a Christ-honoring ministry that has

touched thousands around the world. Each of you is appreciated, and ***we thank our God upon every remembrance of you*** (Philippians 1:3).

ACKNOWLEDGMENTS

---◆---

To my wife Margie, I am grateful. She went through eleven years of our journals, culling out the appropriate stories we have included here. She did not get to see the completion of the project, because the Lord took her Home October 19, 2017.

Our thanks to Shepherds for employing us in the first place. When we finished our years with them, I was seventy-nine years old. They are to be commended for keeping an "old man" on the payroll that long.

To read through these many chapters is a colossal task. To correct all the mistakes this writer makes is even bigger. Laurel Hicks, who graciously helped us with our first book, also took on this second challenge of fine-tuning the book before it was published. Laurel worked at A Beka Book in Pensacola, Florida for over thirty years, and is eminently qualified to edit these pages. We are grateful for her outstanding help.

Many who read our first book, "From a Canoe to a Chevy," were very encouraging when they heard we were going to write another book about our experiences with Shepherds. Thank you for prodding us to keep at it.

Again, thank you, my family members, for your vote of confidence for my taking on this project. It has been more fun than I can ever tell.

I thank my brother Harold, who financed the printing of my two books. His gracious gifts have always been such an encouragement to me. My brother Ernie, in Singapore, also helped with several projects. God called him Home six days before Margie died.

ENDORSEMENT

In these pages you will get to know the heart of a Christian gentleman and his beloved wife as they ministered on behalf of God's most needy saints. I have known Ralph and Margie since I was a child hearing about their missionary work in Brazil. I know from experience that their daily trust in God was genuine and effective. Prepare yourself for a blessing as you read.

Laurel Hicks, Litt.D, editor, A Beka Book (retired)

TIMELINE

- Served as missionaries in Brazil, March 1957 to March 1981

- Pastored First Baptist Church, Ferndale, Washington, October 1981 to July 1999.

- Began ministry as representative for Shepherds in early 2000.

- Finished traveling for Shepherds in November of 2009.

- Worked for Shepherds at our home office until November of 2010.

- Full retirement started in 2011

- Joy Poulson died July 21, 2012

- Margie Poulson died October 19, 2017

TABLE OF CONTENTS

MIRACLE MILES

———◆———

When we began our ministry for Shepherds, we never realized what blessings we would receive. The process of traveling from one church to another prompted us to give this title to our book.

SHEPHERDS WOOD CENTER

Miracle Miles, for God's special people, means so much to us. It seems each trip we planned and made gave us another story. In this book, we desire to share some of those special moments as we traveled the many miles and ministered in churches as Shepherds representatives.

People are fascinating, and the usual and unusual things that happened on our trips are what we want to share with you in these pages. Maybe as we grow older, we see things differently than when we were younger. It seemed to Margie and me that each trip we took to present Shepherds at another church was unique. Perhaps you will agree as you see God's hand upon our trips and meetings.

The residents at Shepherds were the driving force to do this ministry. Our daughter Joy, who was never able to speak or hear what we or others said, motivated us greatly in this pursuit. We rejoice that now in Heaven she hears and sees all and can praise the Lord.

In our visits to Shepherds, the residents inspired us. In these pages, you will be reminded of what some of them taught us by the amazing things they did. Even though they are not named, the incidents are what intrigued us. Some day in the Glory Land, we will meet all of them. What a day of rejoicing that will be.

Shepherds Ministries is in transition, and the Shepherds College is worthy of our praises. We are grateful to have seen the early days of this great adventure when we neared the end of our ministry with Shepherds. Our prayer is that these simply-written stories will bring laughter, tears, joy and thankfulness to you. Psalm 126:3 *The LORD has done great things for us, and we are glad.*

WHAT DO WE DO NOW?

———◆———

T his was the question after our retirement from First
Baptist Church of Ferndale, Washington. The eighteen
years we ministered in this church had greatly blessed us.
With mixed emotions we left, knowing God's timing was right.

FIRST BAPTIST CHURCH—FERNDALE, WA

We had been down this road of uncertainty before. Each
new adventure seemed to be preceded by that gnawing
question: "What do we do now"? Without our knowing what
was about to happen, Dr. Andrew Wood, former president of
Shepherds Home in Union Grove, Wisconsin, communicated

with Shepherds Home about our resignation from the church. He did this mainly because he knew Shepherds Home could benefit greatly by having a western representative in this area. Shepherds responded and contacted us about an interview.

At a Regular Baptist Churches annual conference in Seattle, a meeting was arranged. We met with President William Amstutz, Alan Pick, director of church relations, and some others, to discuss the possibility of a new challenge. After a lengthy interview and an exchange of questions from both sides, we parted.

This proposal was brought to the Shepherds board meeting, and eventually we were invited to attend some meetings at the Home. It was most normal for us to be on the Shepherds campus, because our daughter Joy had been a resident there since she was eight years old.

It was exciting to realize we might be able, in a very small way, to express our gratitude to Shepherds for the many years they cared for Joy. This had enabled us to serve in Brazil and later in a church ministry in Ferndale.

After more interviews and filling out required documents, they accepted us as west coast representative for Shepherds We traveled to churches to represent Shepherds for eleven years, and that was one of the most fulfilling ministries the Lord enabled us to have. We are so thankful God always has a ministry for those who are willing to continue serving. This does not make us special, but reflects the grace of God. He always guided our lives and showed us what He wanted us to do. ***I will instruct you and teach you in the way you should go; I will guide you with My eye.*** (Psalm 32:8

4

NEW EVERY MORNING

We were missionaries in Brazil for almost twenty-five years, and then the Lord changed our ministry. When we returned from Brazil, we spent the next 18 years in the ministry at First Baptist Church, Ferndale, Washington.

In the process of time, God moved us around, and that is what makes the Christian life so exciting. We resigned our pastoral ministry, and Shepherds Home hired us to represent them in eight western states in America. What a joy it was to travel to different churches along the way. It was special for us because our daughter Joy was a long-time resident of that home. It was because of their gracious care for her, that we could continue our ministry in Brazil. Joy, developmentally challenged, lived at Shepherds under the tender loving care that only they can give.

ALAN PICK

DAN DIDONATO

In all our years associated with Shepherds, this was the first time we were going there to be inaugurated into the ministry of representing Shepherds on the west coast. What a thrill to be acquainted with an aspect of Shepherds that was completely new to us. Mr. Al Pick, director of Church Relations, taught us how we would get our meetings, and what we would do as representatives. We also met other representatives with whom we would have special fellowship for the next several years as we met yearly for orientation and instruction concerning our work.

Dr. Amstutz was helpful in giving wise counsel concerning our ministry of representing Shepherds in the churches. We were grateful for his kindness to us as parents of a resident at Shepherds (our daughter Joy), and the important task of representing this ministry in the churches where we would travel. Mr. Dan DiDonato helped us understand the business part of our association with Shepherds, and he was the one who always invited us to the yearly meetings of the representatives. Dan and one of the board members, Jim Edgar, visited our church after we finished our ministry with Shepherds and presented us with a beautiful plaque and letter from Dr. Amstutz regarding our 11 years of service for them. It was very special for us and we will never forget the kindnesses shown us by Shepherds. Lamentations 3:23 ***They are new every morning; Great is Your faithfulness.***

ALL BECAUSE OF JOY

T his is where our story begins. We wondered if we should return to Brazil, our mission field, as Joy was born with developmental disabilities in Iquitos, Peru, in 1959. Because of this, we came back to the States to take her through some medical evaluations. Our son Rawlie was two years older.

FROM A CANOE TO A CHEVY

God providentially opened Shepherds for us, as I wrote in our first book, "From a Canoe to a Chevy." When we left our ministry in Brazil in 1981 and came home, Joy had already been in Shepherds for many years. It was this wonderful home and its president and board that had made our ministry in Brazil possible. We are eternally grateful to God for this place and their kindness in making it possible for us to minister on foreign soil.

After twenty-five years in Brazil, God sovereignly led our home church to call me to be pastor. The First Baptist Church of Ferndale, Washington, had been Margie's church since childhood, and God allowed us to minister to these dear people for 18 years.

At this 18-year mark, we prayed that perhaps God would allow us to terminate our tenure as pastor and lead us into another ministry for our sunset years. Little did we know what was awaiting us "around the corner." Shepherds Ministries invited us to represent them on the west coast. We were with them over a decade. This ministry enriched our lives, and we were able to thank the Lord and Shepherds for the privilege of letting churches and individuals know about this Christ-honoring ministry for individuals with developmental disabilities.

After our years with Shepherds, I wrote our first book, about our ministry in Brazil. That led us to consider a book about our years on the road for Shepherds.

The stories here are a mixture of the fantastic impressions and lessons learned at Shepherds from some of the residents and our ministry in churches as we traveled and told them about Shepherds. However, it is in no way a history of Shepherds Home and its progress through the years. The only resident named in this book is our daughter Joy.

Therefore, it is because of Joy we write these stories. Also, because she lived at Shepherds and we worked for them, here is our story. We will never cease to be amazed at all the incredible things that happened to us while on the road. We pray that the down-to-earth, day-by-day stories of our travels will be a blessing to you. We do it all for His glory and thank Shepherds for giving this opportunity to be a part of their organization for a few years. We are encouraged by Paul's words, *And I thank Christ Jesus our Lord who has enabled me, because He counted me faithful, putting me into the ministry.* (1Ti 1:12)

MAKE UP YOUR MIND

When we first started our travels, we drove our car and stayed in people's homes. We appreciated very much the hospitality shown us. Well-meaning hosts put beautiful bouquets of fresh flowers in our room, which were lovely but disturbing to Margie's allergies. It seemed harder and harder to maintain that kind of schedule.

We decided the time had come for us to begin a new style of travel. We purchased our first truck and fifth wheel trailer from a Christian sales clerk in Everett, Washington. Being "green" at this business, we had much to learn. Our first trailer, an Aljo, was a singlewide and had no push-outs. We purchased both truck and trailer on the same lot. They were a good *team,* and we enjoyed them. I had to get used to driving a Ford 150 and pulling the trailer. We were in Montana on our first trip with this new set-up. We soon learned that the singlewide trailer was too small for us, living in it full time. The space between the couch and the recliner on the other side was so short that our knees practically touched. It was too narrow! After several months of this, we found in Walla Walla, Washington, a fifth wheel that had a push-out.

Life on the road was now a delight with more room. We spent a good deal of time on the road, and our little home away from home was a blessing. We had new lessons to learn about a fifth wheel with a push out. There was more weight involved because of the added room. The trailer interior was very nice, and visitors remarked about it all the time. As time went on, we were conscious of the fact that this trailer, although very nice, was not really an all-weather unit. Traveling in colder climates was a problem, and it was obvious we needed to upgrade. Again, we had to make a decision about another trailer.

Something happened while we were home that was amazing. We studied trailers and looked and looked. While we were doing so, my brother Ernie, missionary in Singapore, gave us a gift with which we purchased a used Ford 250, which was an upgrade. From there we kept looking for a fifth wheel that would be adequate for living in colder climates as we traveled. We did not intend to buy a new one, but with a trailer trade-in, the dealer gave us a good deal. So now we had a new Cougar fifth wheel trailer. It was not quite thirty feet long, but a very nice unit. Pulling it with the Ford 250 was a blessing, and we really sailed over the miles with no problems at all.

FORD 350 & NASH TRAILER

For reasons we will tell you about in another story, and after several years of use, we were in Pasco, Washington, parked at a Baptist Church. Across a large playing field from the church was a Christian RV Sales company. One day, on a whim, we strolled over there and just looked. We glanced at a trailer named Nash. We had never heard of this make before. It is not the same as the car company with that name. This unit had two push-outs, which made it attractive. With the bedroom slide-out, we had more room where I could make my office. We traded in the Cougar and drove away with the Nash. This would be the last fifth wheel we owned, and the best. It was higher off the ground, so we did not tear off the leveling jacks going out of malls and church parking lots, like on other trailers. The arrangements in this trailer were better than those in the Cougar, and they were about the same age. We had many wonderful miles and nights in it. I guess you can say we had finally *made up our mind* and had the trailer that suited us. As we started each trip, we prayed for God's protection and direction along the way. It was almost like Paul's words to the Thessalonians: ***Now may our God and Father Himself and our Lord Jesus Christ, direct our way to you.*** (1Thessalonians 3:11)

FOR SUCH A TIME AS THIS

We had a long relationship with Shepherds because our daughter Joy was a resident there for over 45 years. We thank God daily for the wonderful care she received. In the course of time, changes were inevitable at the Home. We saw changes in leadership, and we understood in part the unbelievable load the board carried to maintain this Christ-honoring home. They have continued throughout these many years and have added Shepherds College, perhaps the only college of its kind in America. By the time this book is printed they will have full accreditation. What a testimony of God's care for this place through the years!

Before we joined Shepherds as representative to the west coast churches, there was a new president of this wonderful organization. Dr. William Amstutz, formerly in church and school ministries, felt God's call to the positon as President of Shepherds in 1998. It was our personal pleasure to meet him when at our interview for the position as representative. A double blessing for us was that his father, Harold Amstutz, was working with the A.B.W.E. mission board under which we went to Brazil in 1957.

Dr. William & Nancy Amstutz

It was a privilege to watch this choice servant take the challenge of leading Shepherds to another level during the years we worked for them. In our yearly meetings, it was a delight to hear his reports, given with enthusiasm and godly sincerity. Besides the numerous things that improved under his tutelage, the Shepherds College must be counted as one of the best. This will certainly go down in educational history. Along with an excellent team, which God enabled, we have seen great results in all areas of the ministry. The Shepherds College website says it best in the opening paragraph:

Shepherds College is the country's leading three-year post-secondary educational program for students with intellectual disabilities. There are very few resources of this kind in the nation, and we are a unique and important option for students looking to take the next step in their education.

We are so proud of Dr. Amstutz's example as he leads this wonderful ministry. His heart of love for the Lord, his intercessory prayer for all phases of the ministry, and the clients and staff over which he presides, are inspirational. Truly God brought him to Shepherds for such a time as this. We agree with Paul in the words of this verse and believe they describe Dr. Amstutz's leadership: **Finally, my brethren, be strong in the Lord and in the power of His might.** (Ephesians 6:10)

ENLARGING OUR BORDERS

―――――◆―――――

When we began our work with Shepherds Baptist Ministries, they assigned us four states where we represented them in the churches: Washington, Idaho, Oregon, and California. In California our responsibility was as far south as San Francisco.

Travel in these four states was a blessing, and telling churches about Shepherds was a privilege. After our first experience with this ministry, I asked Shepherds if we could extend our area of responsibility to all of California. As missionaries, we had been in some of the churches, and we thought they would welcome us back as representatives for Shepherds. It worked out well, and we thoroughly enjoyed ministering in this new area.

As time went on, we decided to request another extension of our geographical responsibilities. I mentioned to Mr. Al Pick, Director of Church Relations at Shepherds, that I used to live in Phoenix. I was wondering if Shepherds would like us to include Arizona in our meetings. They gave permission, and Arizona opened for us. What a joy to travel for Shepherds in the state where I had formerly lived and been a truck driver!

As we traveled in northern California, we noticed the freeway signs pointing to Nevada. We thought it would be nice to schedule a few churches there. We asked Shepherds' permission, and soon we were traveling to a church in that state. We were thankful for the wonderful time we had in Nevada. Our favorite state was Montana. We enjoyed the two or more times we could present Shepherds in many churches in Big Sky Country, Montana.

We received communication from Dan DiDonato at Shepherds, stating he had visited in Alaska and wondered if we would be willing to have some meetings there. We were thrilled with this request. My brother lives in Anchorage, so it was a delight to see him while there. His home was not available to us, because other family members were occupying the bedrooms and garage. However, as we wrote in another chapter, the Dimond Boulevard Baptist Church graciously provided both housing and transportation for us while visiting their state. In all, we represented Shepherds in eight states on the West coast. We had other meetings scheduled, but our service ended with Shepherds when health issues kept us home. What wonderful years those were! We will never forget them, and we thank Shepherds again for the privilege of this rewarding ministry. Paul's desire to visit the Romans expresses our emotions as we traveled for Shepherds in these states. ***That I may come to you with joy by the will of God, and may be refreshed together with you.*** (Romans 15:32)

A MOVING STORY

W e were always thrilled to go to new places and visit churches to tell people about Shepherds. Out in Montana there is a town named Cutbank. How in the world did we ever get to this town? Marla Pick, daughter of Al and Kathy Pick of Union Grove, Wisconsin, taught school there. Mr. Pick is head of Church Relations for Shepherds, and because of Marla, we made contact with the church she attended.

Arriving at the church in a fifth wheel trailer is always challenging. Some churches do not understand how to accommodate people with trailers. It is not easy, and we recognize this. At this church, the best place for us to park the fifth wheel was on the street that paralleled the church. The pastor took our extension cord for electricity through one of the Sunday School classroom windows, over the transit, and plugged it into the socket. Now with electricity we could manage much better. We leveled and secured the trailer in its place. Then we unhooked the Ford truck.

What comes next we did not expect. We noticed an unusual amount of rail traffic very near our spot. In fact, the railroad tracks were quite close to our trailer. We were also parked at one of the major traffic crossings over the tracks. This meant that trains would sound their horns long before approaching the crossing. We later discovered this was the main trunk line from Chicago to Seattle. Therefore, many trains were passing in both directions at regular intervals. Have you already guessed what came next? The sound of the train horns was unbearable. It was impossible to sleep. During the wee hours of the morning I told Margie I would talk to the pastor and move the trailer the next day.

I doubt if people who live there even heard the loud horns. But we were new there, and the deafening horn sounds were just too much. The next day, the pastor kindly directed us to the other church campus just a few blocks away, where we again set up our trailer. This time we plugged the extension cord into an outlet at the parsonage, which was occupied by a church member. We were all set up and enjoying our new place. Margie was preparing lunch when all of a sudden, the lights went out. We had tripped a circuit. We tried to get a response at the door from the occupants, but were unsuccessful. We waited and then waited some more. It was obvious this system would not work for us. I made a decision to break camp and move again. You can see that this is **a moving story**.

I hooked up the laptop, searched for a place to stay, and found one. We drove there, and the manager showed us a place where we could park. This is where we stayed the rest of our short time in Cutbank. We learned we had to adjust to unexpected circumstances. In Christian living, it is good to be prepared for whatever the Lord may bring our way. James tells his readers that to be positive is a good way to travel life's road. **Instead, you ought to say, "If the Lord wills, we shall live and do this or that."** (James 4:15)

RECYCLING OUR LIBRARY

Terminating eighteen years of ministry at First Baptist Church of Ferndale, Washington, was a process. It was obvious that it would take some time to clean out my office so it would be ready for the next pastor.

Years ago when we went to Brazil, we shipped many books there for my ministry there. While in Brazil, we purchased many books in the Portuguese language also. We brought many home with us, because they too, contained resources for sermon preparation. While pastor in Washington, I also added more books to my library. As years passed, modern technology enabled us to include electronic books on the computer. For some, this step is hard, because the "old timers" like to have the books in their hands. I was not one of these, and I welcomed the computer versions of books.

Now the question was, "Where am I going to put all these books?" We did not have room for them in our house. I already had two full bookcases at home. After serious contemplation, we decided that we did not have to keep all these books. A thought came to us, that perhaps students at the Bible School in Ghana, Africa, could use them. Our missionary Iola Boyer served in Wa, Ghana, for over 50 years and translated the Bible into that language. She told us some of the students at the Bible school spoke English also, so our books would help them in their study for the ministry. Iola was happy to hear we desired to donate our books for this purpose.

I got smaller boxes from the grocery store and gradually packed each one carefully. With the addresses clearly printed on each one, we sent them box by box to Ghana. We used some reserved funds to pay the postage and eventually sent 35-40 boxes. It was rewarding to receive words of appreciation from the students; it was a blessing to know that after many years, someone else could benefit from my library.

Because I continued to add to my electronic library, I am still able to teach classes, preach, and study for different messages. The Bible class which I started years ago while pastor at First Baptist in Ferndale, at the Ferndale Senior Activity Center, continues until today. For eleven years, I did not teach the class, because we were on the road representing Shepherds. At some point, they asked if I would like to teach the class again. Therefore, that has been our major event each week and is the largest event at the Ferndale Senior Center, according to the director.

Books meant a lot to the Apostle Paul. Notice what he said here: ***Bring the cloak that I left with Carpus at Troas when you come--and the books, especially the parchments.*** (2Timothy 4:13)

A LAST-MINUTE INVITATION

———◆———

L ife is filled with wonderful things that happen when we least expect them. While speaking to churches about the Shepherds ministries, I often chose the Mark 14 passage about Mary's offering to Jesus. I used this passage to tell about Shepherds residents who were serving the Lord in significant ways.

We were in a church that was new to us, so we looked for the person in charge and then got set up for the service, our normal routine. We found a table, then placed all our literature plus the Shepherds sign at the rear of the display. Then we met with the audio-visual director to get the video queued in for showing at the close of the service.

The service was a blessing. The pastor had a serious back issue and had to lie in a canvas-like lawn-chair to play the guitar--the only music available for the service. I preached my regular message after the introductory comments about Shepherds and then concluded with the Shepherds video. The video was moving, showing this home and its ministry to people with developmental disabilities. The video always leaves one greatly impressed by what God is doing at Shepherds.

After church, we were not able to thank the pastor, because he had to leave the service due to his acute pain. We felt very badly for him but were impressed by the tender care and concern the church folks had for his well-being. Margie and I visited with many folks at the conclusion of the service. Margie was always at the display table, where people took literature and asked questions. When the crowd thinned out, we began to dismantle our display. We got our projector, folded our table, and put everything in the truck.

We were in the Los Angeles area, so after the service our plans were to find a restaurant and then return to our parked trailer, about an hour away. A lady approached us, asking if we had an invitation for lunch. We politely told her that we had no invites. She immediately told us she had nothing planned for lunch that day but my message had touched her and her husband when Jesus said this about Mary's act of worship: *She has done what she could.* (Mark 14:8) By conviction, they invited us to their home. They had a large family, and we are sure this was a sacrifice, but we were convinced it was a spiritual exercise to have us for lunch. She prepared a very delicious meal quickly, and we had a wonderful time. What a lesson this family taught us! They were doing what they could, and this is all God asks of us.

Whenever we ate at the church folks' homes, Margie was always ready to help. She might comfort a fussy baby while the mother prepared lunch, or she would help with setting the table, preparing food, or anything else the hostess needed. After all, Margie had much experience in entertaining as a pastor and missionary's wife, and when she was a teenager her mother had taught her to cook. She got much experience, as her parents entertained almost all the missionaries and special speakers in their home. Her parents were **"given to hospitality."** (Romans 12:13)

A KNEE ACTION EXERCISE

—◆—

O ur trip to present Shepherds at the Baptist church in Silverdale, Washington, was uneventful. We left home in plenty of time to take the ferryboat across the way to the road leading to the church.

Pastor Curt DeGraff greeted us, and we had prayer before the service began. Margie got the display table all set up and attractively arranged. The service went well, and people were very receptive to the message about this wonderful place that ministers to those with developmental difficulties. We were encouraged by the support folks gave to this ministry.

While we were on our way to this meeting, Dan DiDonato from Shepherds had called to ask how we were doing. We told him we were on our way to give a Shepherds presentation in Silverdale. He was surprised, because he understood I was to have double knee surgery the next day. I assured him that surgery was not until the next morning, so we wanted to get in another meeting before that. We finished the service, got on the ferry, and were home just before midnight.

Early next morning, we checked into the hospital. Margie stayed with me until they rolled me into surgery. All went well. Dr. Thorpe has operated on many knees, and we were pleased with how things turned out. Recovery went well, and therapy was normal. I admit the knee flexion was severe, and perhaps I did not tolerate it as well as I should, but we made it through okay. In therapy, there is a lot of ***knee action exercise***.

Because of my age, they allowed me to transfer to the hospital's south campus and do in-house therapy there. Before moving, I remember Dr. Thorpe examining the zipper-like stitches on both knees. As he looked at them, I asked if he was admiring his artwork (those stitches). Without a word, he glanced heavenward and softly spoke these words: "How great Thou art." What a blessing to have a Christian doctor! Yes, I had both knees done at one time, and I would choose to do it that way again. I have no regrets for having made this decision.

While recovering at the south campus, I looked up and saw Dan DiDonato from Shepherds. He had come from his home in New Jersey to visit me. I will never forget that loving gesture and the beautiful card and fruit basket given me. It was my privilege to be a part of an organization that treated their employees superbly. We had a great visit that day. A part of this verse spoke volumes to me as Dan visited me: ***And be kind to one another, tenderhearted....*** (Ephesians 4:32) I trust we will all learn that wonderful trait as we deal with each other.

A FASCINATING ENTRANCE TO GLACIER NATIONAL PARK

W e parked our fifth wheel trailer at the Lake Louise Baptist Campground near Kalispell, Montana. On June 29, 2001, we had a special invitation. Pastor Jerry Buchanan and his wife asked us to accompany them on a sightseeing trip on the North Fork Drive. We met them at the First Baptist Church of Columbia Falls parsonage, where he was pastor.

We left with Pastor Jerry and his wife Debbie in their car, traveling the North Fork of the Flathead River, to Lake Bowman. The scenery along the way was spectacular. From Polebridge to Lake Bowman is six miles of bumpy, rough, unpaved road. For this reason, it is less visited than the other attractions in Glacier National Park.

Arriving at the lake, I took many pictures that later appeared on our website, which I updated weekly. The Buchanans had packed a delicious lunch for us which we enjoyed while viewing this beautiful lake. Several other visitors were at the lake's edge also, taking in all the beauty.

On the trip to Lake Bowman, we stopped at a quaint place called Polebridge Mercantile. This Mercantile and the settlement of Polebridge are actually the gateway to the northwest entrance of famous Glacier National Park. We learned that this community is named for the log bridge that formerly connected the North Fork Road in Glacier National Park to Montana Secondary Highway 486, over the North Fork of Flathead River. Polebridge lies near the Canadian border. The uniqueness of Polebridge is the fact there is no electricity in this area. They designate it as electricity-free. It is powered by generators. The Mercantile, which serves all kinds of pastries and breads, is an enormous attraction at Polebridge.. It is famous for these delicious items. Debbie Buchanan bought some delicious chocolate chip cookies for us to enjoy at the lake. We learned why they are so famous. They were scrumptious!

This trip into the remote entrance of Glacier National Park was a treat we will never forget. We appreciated the Buchanans' thoughtfulness in inviting us to this unforgettable journey into the northland of Montana. The fellowship we enjoyed with them reminds us of Paul's words to the Philippians: .... *for your fellowship in the gospel from the first day until now.* (Philippians 1:5) We appreciated their invitation to spend time with them and enjoy Polebridge and its uniqueness. Have you done this with your friends?

A CHURCH WE WILL NEVER FORGET

W e never ceased to be amazed, as we traveled for Shepherds, at all the delightful experiences the Lord allowed us to have. It was our first time to visit the town of Carpentaria, California. With the help of maps and previous phone calls to the church, we finally located the Carpentaria Valley Baptist Church. Arriving in time to set up before dark, we stopped in front of the church and went to the church office. The kind secretary showed us the spot where we could park our rig, and we spent most of that afternoon getting parked and settled. There are so many things to do in setting up, but we had a certain routine which we followed, and we were glad when it was done. This set-up always included the DirecTV satellite dish placement and focus. Sometimes it went quickly, and at other times, it took a long time.

Later we met Pastor Button, who gave us a tour of the facility. He gave us interesting information about the building in which we were standing. The church had a long history, and the most fascinating aspect of the story was the present building. The church actually started in Santa Barbara, California, in the early 1960's, and was later moved to Carpentaria. They used the Women's Clubhouse of Carpenteria for their meeting place until 1971, when the congregation was able to purchase the current property. Under the leadership of Pastor Dan M. Caldwell, the 70-member congregation dedicated the Victorian church building on Sunday evening, March 19, 1971.

At this point, the story gets very interesting. A Methodist church built the current building in 1880 in Santa Barbara, California. In November 1892, they cut it into three sections and moved it along the coastline on horse-drawn flatbed wagons twelve miles to its current location at the corner of Maple Avenue and Eighth Street. The original stained-glass windows, memorializing prominent pioneers, survive to the present day with minimal damage.

CARPINTERIA VALLEY BAPTIST CHURCH

One would have to stand in the sanctuary and gaze out through those marvelous stained-glass windows to appreciate the beauty of this building. We were in awe, trying to think how it must have been to witness this church's coming together after those horse-drawn wagon trips from Santa Barbara. We looked at that beautiful piece of history, and give thanks to the Lord for the unique story of its existence. Truly, we can relate to Habakkuk as he penned these words: ***But the LORD is in His holy temple. Let all the earth keep silence before Him*** (Habakkuk 2:20)

A BRAZILIAN EVENING IN CALIFORNIA

$$\cdot\!=\!\!\blacklozenge\!\!=\!\cdot$$

The Christian life is very special. You never know what may happen in a day. One Sunday we ministered for Shepherds at Calvary Baptist Church in Anaheim, California. At the close of the Sunday morning service, as we met many people and enjoyed their fellowship, a woman approached us, identifying herself as a former missionary to Brazil. When she named the field where she served, we immediately recognized it and knew missionaries in that area.

This former missionary invited us to a meal the next week. At the appointed time, we met at the place she had chosen. The rather large building had a sign written in English, but it revealed to us that we were in for a treat that night. The sign read "Brazilian Barbecue Buffet." When our host arrived, we entered this lovely restaurant and the fun began. The receptionist, knowing we were Americans, spoke to us in English. We answered her in Portuguese, which was a surprise to her. From then on, it was wonderful going down the buffet tables looking at all the scrumptious dishes, especially the meats for which Brazil is known. They had steaks, barbecued ribs, feijoada, etc. They also had dried salted meat, which is very popular with Brazilians. It was good to enjoy special Brazilian fruits we had come to love, and for dessert, they had a varied selection, but we especially enjoyed their custard with burnt sugar topping.

We had such fun talking to the waiters and servers in Portuguese! They wanted to know where we had been in Brazil, and in turn, we wanted to know where their homes were. Following the typical Brazilian courtesies, they complimented us on our use of the Portuguese language. Little did they know how much we loved Brazil. They usually exaggerated, telling us how well we spoke Portuguese. That is debatable, but at least we do know our way around in the Brazilian language.

All the tantalizing foods displayed in impeccable order on the serving tables were a remarkable sight. Salads, special fruit sections, and desserts were all awaiting our enjoyment at this fine restaurant. Brazilian bread is also necessary along with the meal, and it is delicious. We finished our meal with the famous *cafezinho,* a demitasse cup of Brazilian coffee, brewed to perfection as only Brazilians can do.

That evening our friend, Dorothy da Silva, and her daughter truly entertained us royally at this very elegant place. We spent the evening chatting with Dorothy and her daughter, reminiscing of former days spent in the amazing land of Brazil. We did not soon forget this wonderful treat. Even though we have heard of similar restaurants in the Seattle, Washington, area, we have never frequented them. Therefore, this California experience was very special to us. After having spent almost twenty-five years abroad, it was a privilege beyond our fondest expectation to have a Brazilian meal in California. Margie and I really appreciated the kindness shown us that evening. We remember this when we read Paul's words*: **In everything give thanks; for this is the will of God in Christ Jesus for you.*** (1Thessalonians 5:18)

A FIFTY-YEAR REUNION

---◆---

L ong ago when we were students at BIOLA, we had many friends, and in our classes we had great fellowship with our fellow students. During the four years we spent at school, we made many special friends. In reality, four years went by quickly. For us, graduation was the end of this close day-by-day relationship, and each student went his own way. We lost track of some people, but through the BIOLA magazine we were able to keep up with others.

One of these graduates went to a town in California and had a vibrant ministry for many years. Off and on, we heard reports of his ministry, and it was a blessing to hear how God was using him.

We had made previous schedules for churches in California, and eventually the time came for us to go to a church in Redding, California. We arrived early and set up our display table. We got everything settled with the audiovisual man for showing a video at the end of the evening service. Now it was time to wait for people to arrive.

We met folks who already knew a lot about Shepherds, because their church was acquainted with its work. What a blessing to talk with them and bring updates on the ministry. At a certain point, while folks were gathering for the meeting, I looked up and saw the pastor coming down the church aisle. You know very well that the years change us, but when I saw him, it was as if I remembered him in the classrooms at BIOLA. We met, hugged, and reminisced about the good old days at school. It had been fifty years since we had seen each other. Imagine all the history that took place during these years. That evening was very special for us. The pastor greeted us warmly and spoke emotionally of our years together in school many years ago. I thought of what Paul said to the Roman Christians. I am not sure we were able to do what he did, but we did yearn to be in this church. ***For I long to see you, that I may impart to you some spiritual gift, so that you may be established.*** (Romans 1:11)

A FUNERAL FOR A DEAR FRIEND

W e returned from a long Shepherd's itinerary in California, and it was so good to be home again. A dear friend of ours, Paul Friberg, died, and his family asked me to have his service. Our acquaintance with Paul, his wife Norma, and their children began a long time ago.

Paul grew up in Ferndale, and in later years, his parents attended our church. Paul was married, had two daughters, and started an air conditioning business. When we were missionaries in Brazil, we had been in their home in Wenatchee, Washington, on various occasions. After we began our Shepherds ministry, we kept contact with them, even visiting when Paul's health started to decline. Before all this, Paul, while in Wenatchee, did air conditioning work for big apple warehouses. During this time, he came to Ferndale and installed a central heating system in our home. We will never forget his gracious gift to us. Paul was a hard worker. He and his wife also did so much for their church in Wenatchee.

After years in Wenatchee, they retired, "sort of," to Spokane. There they were involved in their new home church. They also had a lovely home, which he remodeled. We were impressed with his mechanical talents and the machines he built to help with projects in his shop. One was a motorized machine to help him park their trailer in the special spot he had for it at his home.

We were saddened when we heard his health was failing. On one of our trips to eastern Washington, we stopped, visited, and had prayer with him. Prior to this, when he was feeling better, he had spent hours helping me find some special things for our trailer. We always appreciated Paul's enthusiasm, humor, and love for family and the Lord. When we received the news of his death, we reacted as anyone would. We hated to lose a dear friend but were joyous his pain was gone. He was with the Lord. I was honored to have his service. In between our Shepherd's meetings, we drove from Ferndale to Spokane to conduct the service. It was always easier to preach the funeral for one who was a faithful servant of the Lord, and this is what Paul was. We still have communication with his dear wife Norma, who has filled her life with service for others just as she and Paul always did. What a reminder this verse is of Paul and his love and service for the Lord: ***Then I heard a voice from heaven saying to me, "Write: 'Blessed are the dead who die in the Lord from now on.'" "Yes," says the Spirit, "that they may rest from their labors, and their works follow them."*** (Revelation 14:13)

A MYSTERIOUS PAINT JOB

I had to go alone this time over Snoqualmie Pass on Interstate 90 in Washington State. Margie had an important doctor's appointment that she could not postpone. We always enjoyed traveling together, so it was hard for both of us to be alone. Pulling our new Cougar fifth wheel went smoothly all the way to the top of the pass.

A little past the summit, I pulled over to check the tires on the truck and trailer. When I went around to the passenger side of the trailer, I was shocked. From about three feet or more up from the ground, the entire side of the truck and trailer was white with fresh, dripping paint. To this day, we have never discovered what could have caused this unbelievable thing to happen. There were no construction zones, and no flagman stopped me or asked me to slow down. That will remain a mystery forever.

Further down the road, when I pulled over into the off-pavement area, I heard a thud and wondered what had happened. I soon discovered I needed Margie with me. She always made sure the stairs were in place and the door was shut. This time, I had gone inside the trailer to use the bathroom, and upon exiting had not closed the steps. When I pulled over, I hit a safety pole about four feet high that had reflectors. They help motorists gauge their position on the highway, especially in inclement or snowy weather conditions.

With that thud, I had wrecked the three-step ladder. I was sick about it, but charged it to carelessness. I was not paying attention to all the details needed when traveling with a trailer. I needed Margie.

A biblical concept kept going through my mind that day. James talks about those who need wisdom and how they can ask God and He will give it. I needed it that day, and so I prayed, as James teaches, that I wanted the Lord to help me resolve this issue of the paint and now broken steps.

About sixty-five miles over the mountain, I stopped in Ellensburg for gas. As I was holding the hose filling the tanks, I glanced over the field and saw a building I had never seen before. In big, black, bold letters, the sign read "Truck Washing." Immediately I thought that could be the Lord's answer of wisdom for which I had sought in prayer after seeing the messy paint job on the truck and trailer an hour earlier.

I pulled the truck over to the washing place, and the attendant cordially greeted me, asking how he could help. After I told him my story, he suggested we run the truck and trailer through the washer and see what would happen. We did, and when it came through, every bit of ugly paint was gone. I could hardly believe it. I learned a good lesson. I had not trusted the Lord as I should. The man said if I had waited 15 minutes longer, the paint would never have come off. The Lord is good!

However, our story does not end there. What about the stairs I broke? Remembering a big RV store on the way to my destination, I stopped to see if they had a step on hand. The place I stopped was a dealer for the trailer we had, and in their parts department he had one unit left in his inventory. I purchased that, was very happy, and thanked the Lord for His provision.

The next day in Boise, Idaho, I removed the old steps and, after hours of work, replaced them with the new ones. The Lord helped me, because with two artificial knees I was not too keen in putting weight on them for this repair. The Lord gave wisdom again for ideas to accomplish this without hurting myself.

That was quite a trip. Our son drove Margie to Boise two days later in our car, left her, and returned to his home in Stanwood. Thankfully, we never had these problems again. However, James is so practical in his instruction in any situation in which we find ourselves unable to figure out what to do. ***If any of you lacks wisdom, let him ask of God, who gives to all liberally and without reproach, and it will be given to him.*** (James 1:5)

A HOME FOR BRAZILIAN CURIOS

O ur good friends Art and Elaine McCleary were working at the U.S. Center for World Missions in Pasadena, California. This large campus housed many different ministries, and our friend Art was the business manager. Elaine worked with a very special lady in one department dealing with **everything missions.** For instance, this branch of the Center would provide table settings for missionary conferences or banquets. They were always in quest of more material to use at such gatherings.

Margie and I were constantly on the look-out for places to park our fifth wheel trailer while representing Shepherds in churches. We had a scheduled meeting at Trinity Baptist Church in Pasadena. Because we knew the McClearys, I asked Art about the possibility of parking somewhere on the facility. He inquired and reported they had a spot for us. What a joy to back into this very nice gated and secure place!

Prior to coming to Pasadena, we had learned that the U.S. Center for World Missions needed curios from the mission field. Margie and I asked our family if they wanted some of these reminders from Brazil. They took very few items, and we packed the rest, a lot of things, and hauled them to Pasadena. I remember going through a couple of barrels of Brazilian artifacts. We could not just hand these items to Elaine; they had to be identified so they would know the

39

story behind each one. I meticulously took pictures, labeled them, and wrote a description of each item. Even while we were there on campus, the ladies in this department, Elaine McCleary and Judy Van Lewan, were busy properly labeling the curios and filing a description of each one.

Later, we visited this department and were impressed by how well they had categorized and organized the display. They thanked us profusely for our great gift to the Center. It was a blessing to find someone who could use these items. We had wondered many times what we would do with them. What a relief to have a place where they could be used repeatedly for occasions where they were needed. The day we visited, we had the honor of meeting Dr. Ralph D. Winter, founder of the U.S. Center for World Mission (USCWM), William Carey International University, and the International Society for Frontier Missiology. While there we had a short visit with him and were happy to have this opportunity. As we reflect on God's goodness in the trivial things of life, like a place to park a four-ton fifth wheel trailer, and a place where our Brazilian artifacts could be used, we can only agree with Paul in what he said. *...distributing to the needs of the saints, given to hospitality.* (Romans 12:13)

A HONEY OF A DEAL

—————◆—————

While we were ministering in the Brawley, California, area, Dick and Karen Ashurst invited us for a meal. Mrs. Ashurst's sister was a resident at Shepherds, and Mr. Ashurst served on the Shepherds board. We enjoyed spending the evening in their home.

After a delectable meal and great visit, Dick invited us to his place of business so we would have a better idea of what he did. Dick is in the bee pollination business. There is much more to this work than I ever realized. We started in his retail shop, which he promptly told us was the byproduct of his pollination business: honey. There was a lot of honey. His son was in charge of this aspect of their work. The store was very interesting, with just about anything you can imagine sold in a place that raises bees for a living. They sold honey in small and large amounts and in different forms. On display was honey in the comb and many other forms. We were also impressed with all the items made from beeswax for sale. They seemed to be endless.

From the store, we went to the processing rooms, where they extracted honey from the combs. The processing machines, a marvel of engineering, and all the related processes in the plant, were very interesting. As we stood in the main room with the rich smell of honey everywhere, I could not help but think of God's goodness in allowing man to use

41

these little creatures in such amazing ways. I even glanced down and saw a huge Black Widow spider calmly sitting in her web, just a few inches off the floor. After all, we were in desert country, where these spiders abound.

Mr. Ashurst took us to the back of his plant, where we saw some of his semi-trucks parked. These trucks transported beehives to distant locations for the pollination process. At peak demand, he said that five semi-trucks would leave his warehouse nightly, headed for diverse places in California. This was truly impressive. Imagine a semi-truck loaded with beehives. That is a lot of bees! Later, he told us he needed to get some more queen bees, and I asked how he did that. He said the bee business is very well organized, and he could purchase a queen bee for fifteen dollars. Imagine that, a tiny insect for fifteen dollars, amazing!

For years, I have given a series, along with Bible studies, on **God's Handiwork in Nature.** I never cease to be amazed at the complexity of a bee. Mr. Ashurst helped me add more to my file about this interesting insect. The word honey occurs many times in the Bible. One reference reminds me of something very important each of us should never forget. **How sweet are Your words to my taste, Sweeter than honey to my mouth!** (Psalm 119:103) I pray God's Word, the Bible will always be sweet to us.

A CARD THAT MADE A LONG TRIP

Through the years, we made many friends. In our church in Ferndale, a couple loved our ministry for Shepherds. They prayed faithfully for us and were generous financially. Margie and I were on the road months at a time. Al and Norma Hickinbotham were the best at giving practical things to their friends. We will always remember the way they helped us.

MOUNT BAKER

One day they came by our house and we had a nice visit. Before they left, they handed us an envelope. After they left, we opened it and found a gift card for Old Country Buffet. It was a very practical gift, as we ate often there on our trips.

Around the country, this chain of restaurants had different names. It was a practical place to eat, because Margie, who has many allergies, could choose from the wide variety of food. We found these buffets by doing searches on our computer as we traveled.

Upon receiving the card, we did not know how much money it was. At our first stop in another state, I asked the cashier about its value. We were stunned at how much it was worth, and it lasted a long time in our Shepherds travels. We also purchased senior discount cards, which gave us much better prices.

Al and Norma were very special to us. Some people like to give outright gifts of money; others prefer to do it the way they did. Their generous hearts were always a blessing to us. They are both in Heaven now, but precious memories flood our hearts as we think of them. This verse from the Old Testament pretty well sums up this couple's lives: ***But a generous man devises generous things, and by generosity, he shall stand.*** (Isaiah 32:8)

A DENTAL DISASTER

W e have never had an experience like this. It all began while on our ministry trip in Stockton, California. Margie got an alert warning from one of her teeth that something was wrong. When in a city where you do not know your way around very well, the best thing is to ask for help. That we did, and Pastor Einer told us that he no longer needed a dentist but remembered a place that perhaps could help us. He gave directions to this office, and we went there. The place was closed, so we pursued the name on the Internet with our laptop computer and found the new address.

We were mighty happy to find a place. We called, made an appointment, and on that day, we were there. We checked in and did all the preliminary requirements prior to having the dentist check Margie. We noticed that the male receptionist was busy on the phone giving what seemed to be instructions to someone who was trying to find this place. We waited a long time only to discover that the person trying to find our location was the dentist who would take care of Margie. Apparently, he was coming from Los Angeles or some other distant town and did not know the proper route to get to the destination. The receptionist finally got him to Stockton and the place where we were waiting.

At this juncture, things were beginning to seem strange to us. Why would a dentist be coming from such a distance?

Why was the receptionist so absorbed in this pursuit that he ignored the patients? They told us that a pre-pay require-ment was clinic policy. So, I had to pay for Margie's work before the doctor even looked at her. I objected, saying that when I buy things in a store, I get them together, go to the cashier, and pay. Well, that's not the way this transaction worked. We had never seen this arrangement before.

The dentist saw Margie, took x-rays, and soon discovered she needed a root canal. At this point we were wondering if even before this, he had determined he would do a root canal. We were very leery, to say the least. To make mat-ters worse, during his exam, Margie's crown fell off. He also said her tooth was abscessed. He had messed with the tooth plenty, and put a dam in to help control the bleeding. Now I had the hassle of getting a refund for the root canal, which they did not perform. I asked to speak to the bookkeeper and registered my disapproval of their system. Finally, with my credit card they entered the information to request a refund to our account. The dentist wrote a prescription for medica-tion, and we went to Walgreens to get it filled.

That night Margie had a horrible time. I called the clinic that had messed things up, and they called the dentist, who ordered her to suspend the medication. He saw her again and removed the sutures and said the plug (dam) had dis-appeared. He would have to redo it. This required another anesthetic, which was hard on Margie. We then sought other counsel about an antibiotic that Margie could tolerate.

At the church we attended while in Stockton, we became acquainted with a doctor and his wife who fellowshipped there. I called him for counsel, because we were desperate. He suggested we call Margie's dentist in Ferndale and get the name of the anesthetic she could tolerate. This I did, and he in the interim found another clinic where Margie could per-haps get help. This new doctor was so kind and helpful. He said she would definitely have to have her tooth removed by a dental surgeon. He scheduled the whole thing. Dr. Geo removed it, and all went well.

Doctor Geo, whom we had never met, took a real interest in her situation and completed the task but never charged a dime. We were overwhelmed. He was so very kind, and we presented him with the well-known Shepherd's book entitled "Child of My Heart." Margie and I felt like Paul must have felt when he told the Philippian church about Timothy: ***For I have no one like-minded, who will sincerely care for your state.*** (Philippians 2:20) Our doctor friend in Stockton and that kind dental surgeon certainly cared for us, and we are eternally grateful to them. Doctor Geo said he would not charge us because he was so ashamed of a dentist who took advantage of us and did such a bad job.

A GOOD SIGN

———◆———

W hen Pastor and Mrs. Einer answered a call to Freemont, California, to pastor a church, we contacted them, and they invited us to present the Shepherds ministry.

MARGIE AND FRIEND BY DISPLAY

It was a thrill, because we had had such a wonderful experience staying on the church property when they were in Stockton, California. At Freemont, we had a full hookup, and it was wonderful. We hooked up, settled in, and looked forward to the first service on Wednesday night. There was a large circle of chairs where the folks first met for Bible study.

Because there were not very many, I decided to have them introduced themselves, and I tried very hard to memorize their names. At the close of the meeting, I was able to make the rounds and name each one. They were surprised. I liked to do this, and it helped keep my mind active.

The church had a deaf ministry, and two ladies who worked in it attended the regular church services. We learned later that Joanie was a signer for the deaf church, including musical numbers. We enjoyed watching the process of interpreting hymns. One evening we treated these ladies to a meal and then took them home. There, Joanie got out her music and showed us how she uses sign language to interpret some beautiful songs. The rhythmic motions she made to interpret hymns was special. What a great gift!

Through the years, we have known several whose ministry was with the deaf. It is a specialized field of service. We understand there are different types of languages and methods used to communicate with the deaf. We laud all who are in this ministry. God has much to say about the deaf. *In that day, the deaf shall hear the words of the book, and the eyes of the blind shall see out of obscurity and out of darkness.* (Isaiah 29:18)

I ADMIT IT

I was a truck driver for the state of Arizona after high-school graduation, and I admit that backing a trailer was the thing hardest for me. That never did change then or when we represented Shepherds.

For some reason, the back-up process never came easy. I always knew I could get the unit into the place assigned to us, but easy maneuvering of the rig was never there. Every church we visited we normally had to back into the designated spot. Only rarely were we able to drive forward into a spot.

In some tight situations, I had to spend a lot of time juggling the rig into its place for the night. I accepted with gratitude lessons from seasoned truck drivers, but I never really seemed to catch on. It seemed that some of the worst possible scenarios were presented to me to challenge my lack of expertise in backing. In Spokane, at the home of our dear friends, the Bowmans, we had a wonderful spot alongside their garage. We stayed there many times and had water and electric hook up, but weekly had to travel a few miles to a dump station. Going out was a breeze, but the return trip was always a dreadful experience, backing the trailer. Living in a residential area required special caution because of traffic along the road. To make it more challenging, the driveway was on an incline, so I had to drive it backwards up the grade into the spot. I was always relieved when that job was over.

My biggest challenge was always at home in Ferndale. It took a long time to maneuver the trailer alongside our house onto the nice cement slab that two churchmen, Al Hickinbotham and John Harder, had made for the trailer. It was so hard to miss the corner eves trough of the house and get the trailer plumb with the house and safely on its pad. I confess, one time it was so hard to coordinate the distance correctly from that corner, which stuck out at me every time we tried to park, that I hit it and caused a real problem. Fortunately, for some reason unknown to me, it hardly scratched the beautiful surface of the trailer, but it bent the corner trough out of whack. I went into the garage, got a sledgehammer and ladder, and gave that trough a healthy blow, which freed the trailer. Never again did I have that problem. It taught me a great lesson: that I should take extra care in the backing process. Even though Paul was discussing and teaching another lesson, this verse surely speaks to me about my problem of backing. What do you think? ***Brethren, I do not count myself to have apprehended; but one thing I do, forgetting those things which are behind and reaching forward to those things which are ahead***, (Philippians 3:13)

TEN THOUSAND MILES FROM HOME

In my famous belated trip to Singapore for my brother's birthday, something happened that was very special. We had a wonderful time visiting, and catching up on many common interests we share as brothers. We went to many restaurants, and at each one, we had to accustom ourselves to Asian food, which in its own way is delicious.

Singapore hospitality is outstanding. We had never really experienced such a variety of visits and cordialities as we did in that city. It seemed that Sunday was a good day for such things, because most people did not work on the weekend. My brother, his wife Verda, and their goddaughter, Siang, have their share of Sunday visits. In the morning, they met friends at church, and after lunch people from different churches dropped by for a visit. This was normal.

While we were there, my brother and his wife invited several people to their home on Sunday evening. Ernie and Siang had planned for me to show the Shepherds video and say a few words of introduction. I enjoyed talking about the wonderful home where Joy lived a long time. That evening I spoke, giving a brief history of the ministry and telling what Margie and I did representing the home in churches. The folks were extremely attentive and, as usual, asked questions. The surprise of the evening was when my brother and Siang gave me checks totaling way over a thousand dollars, their gifts to Shepherds for this fine ministry. Little did we dream that ten thousand miles from home, we would give a Shepherds presentation and receive such a generous money gift for Shepherds. All we could do was praise the Lord for His goodness to Shepherds. ***Blessed be the God and Father of our Lord Jesus Christ, who has blessed us with every spiritual blessing in the heavenly places in Christ.*** (Ephesians 1:3)

A QUAINT UPSTAIRS CHURCH SERVICE

$$\begin{array}{c} \bullet\!\!\!\cdot\!\!\!=\!\!\!=\!\!\!=\!\!\!\blacklozenge\!\!\!=\!\!\!=\!\!\!=\!\!\!\cdot\!\!\!\bullet \end{array}$$

Cut Bank, Montana, appears to be out in the middle of nowhere as you travel across this great state. We were ministering in Cut Bank Community Church, and after the morning service, Pastor Joe and his wife Michelle treated us to lunch. It was very good, and we enjoyed our fellowship with them. We were on a tight schedule that day because Pastor Joe wanted us to present the Shepherds ministry to a group of believers in a town called Essex, which was over 70 miles away from Cut Bank. We had come through this town on our way to Cut Bank, not knowing there was a gospel ministry there.

Arriving in Essex, we went to the place designated for the church service. To our surprise, we parked in front of a building that had a paramedic sign above the entry door. To the right was a larger door where they parked the 911 truck. We made our way up a narrow stairway that took us to a small upstairs room, where I set up for our presentation. A good group of folks assembled for the service in the limited space. We had a wonderful time as folks sang heartily and gave splendid attention to our presentation. Even though the audio did not work on their video machine, people strained their ears and heard a muffled narration of our video. Oh, how I wished we had brought the machine we always used, but they assured us it was not necessary.

After the meeting, the church folks had planned a snack time, which was very nice and welcomed at midafternoon. Soon we were on our way back to Cut Bank, praising the Lord for the wonderful opportunity to present the Shepherds ministry. The people showed keen interest in what God was doing with this wonderful home. Even though the application was different in Jesus' day, when He gave this command, we enjoyed doing in Cut Bank what He asked us to do. And He said to him or her, ***Go into all the world and preach the gospel to every creature.*** (Mark 16:15) It was wonderful to preach the gospel in Essex, Montana, that Sunday afternoon, even in a garage where they park the ambulance and answer 911 calls.

SHUTTLE DIPLOMACY

M ost churches have special services at Christmas time. Because of this, we seldom scheduled Shepherds meetings during that part of December. Every once in a while, it was nice going home to our family and church in Ferndale, Washington.

Sometimes when we were closer to home, we drove our truck, but in more distant locations we used the airlines. While parked at the U.S. Center for World Missions in Pasadena, California, we investigated the possibility of getting a ride to the airport, which would help us greatly. We found a company that came to pick-up points and took passengers to the airport. It was highly organized, and they kept a close vigil on prospective passengers. Also, they alerted us often of their pick-up time.

Unlike many things in this life, the company we used was punctual. And I mean it was very punctual. The morning of our departure we were at the pickup point before 4:24, a time the company had set for us. This was near the location we parked our trailer. At the right time, the shuttle bus arrived, loaded our baggage, and we were off. I noticed a sign on the bus window stating that if they were not on time, the company would pay the passage. I glanced at my watch as we were leaving: the time was 4:24. I was amazed

We used the time going to the Bob Hope airport in Glendale, California, to witness to the driver. He was a very kind gentleman. We pray he listened to what we said and made a decision for Christ. Our son met us at the Seattle-Tacoma,

56

Washington airport and drove us home. We had a wonderful time at home and then returned to continue our Shepherds meetings. Our son drove us to the airport, and the shuttle took us from the airport to the U.S. Center for World Mission. It is interesting that after all these years, we still receive regular e-mail propaganda from this shuttle company. Have you ever thought that God was punctual? I really believe He is always on time, and He emphasizes the importance of NOW. ***Behold, now is the accepted time; behold, now is the day of salvation.*** (II Corinthians 6:2)

A SURPRISE ENDING

◆

Traveling to a church located near the main road leading to Mt. Rainier National Park was always a blessing to us. The Orting Community Baptist Church, whose pastor is Dale Gore, always greeted us warmly. On our first visit to this church, we presented the Shepherds ministry during Sunday School and the evening service. The people were ready to ask pertinent questions about Shepherds, and we tried to answer them in a way that would be honoring to Shepherds and the Lord. In the morning service, I normally preached a message, using Shepherds residents as illustrations. This was always a blessing to those attending.

Pastor and Mrs. Gore were gracious hosts, and lunchtime in their home was special. This couple, dedicated to the ministry, saw God's hand of blessing upon the work, and their new building was proof. We gathered for the evening service, where we talked more about the Shepherds ministry and concluded with a very powerful video. This was about the work done to develop each resident to reach his or her greatest potential. The stories were illuminating and inspirational. We learned long ago that the residents taught us much more than we taught them.

After the meeting, we closed our normal way, and then pastor Gore stepped to the microphone. He suggested that the congregation share what they had learned about

Shepherds during our presentations that day. No pastor had ever done this in our years with Shepherds. What followed was very heart-warming and emotional. One by one, people stood to voice their appreciation for this home where Christ is exalted. In diverse ways, the folks were moved by the simple stories we gave. We perceived that some folks had had no idea that intellectually challenged people could do what the residents at Shepherds did. Margie and I learned this as we visited Shepherds each year for our briefings and updates.

Pastor Gore concluded the evening service that night with a heart-warming endorsement of the Shepherds ministry, and that the update we gave of Shepherds was a blessing to them. We left exhilarated and spiritually uplifted with the tremendous reception we had received from this church and pastor. It was encouraging to see a pastor who stimulated his congregation to think about what we had spoken throughout the day and apply this in their lives. As I said, we had never witnessed anything like this before. This taught us a great lesson. Ever since, we have tried to take very personally what goes on in each service and apply it in our own lives. A precious verse from Jeremiah expresses the ministry of Shepherds home in Union Grove, Wisconsin: *I will set up shepherds over them who will feed them; and they shall fear no more, nor be dismayed, nor shall they be lacking, says the LORD*. (Jeremiah 23:4)

STANDING IN THE HALLWAY

Our trips to Shepherds were always a blessing. The residents were so cheery, and they all knew who we were. As we passed a room, one would ask, "Are you Joy Poulson's parents?" The individual loving care given to Joy and all her colleagues impressed us greatly. On Sundays, the counselor in charge combed and curled each lady's hair, using a curling iron, and then spray. Some liked a squirt of perfume also. Wearing their best dresses, the women looked very nice as they went to chapel.

As we visited Joy, sometimes we would have to leave to attend a representatives meeting. Because Joy never spoke, we had no meaningful way of knowing what she was thinking most of the time. She also could not hear, because she was deaf. By her actions we knew she was taking things in. Those who cared for her told us over and over again how intelligent she was, and we agreed.

One day upon returning from another meeting, we went to unit 8, where Joy lived. We saw someone standing against the wall down the hallway. Getting closer, we realized it was Joy. We had left her, and now she had come into the hall and was looking intently to see if we were going to return. We had noticed on several other trips and occasions she did this. She must have been curious to know if we were going to return, because she was waiting in the hallway.

It was never easy to say our goodbyes before returning to Washington. We would tear up and wondered what she was thinking way down inside. Never once did we question God's wisdom in giving us Joy. The Scriptures say it so well. ***Behold, children are a heritage from the LORD, The fruit of the womb is a reward.*** (Psalm 127:3) Joy was God's special gift to us for a reason. We were and are indebted to Shepherds for the long-time care they gave her so we could minister.

THAT SUITS ME

One of Shepherds 50-year anniversary banquets was held at First Baptist Church in Hemet, California. A dear couple, friends of ours for several years, invited us to ride with them to Hemet for the occasion. Gerry and Gail Chehock made reservations for us and came to Fremont to get us. The trip to Hemet was several hours, and we enjoyed the time as we traveled with this dear couple. They were supporters of Shepherds and had a keen interest in the ministry.

We stopped for lunch at Marie Calendars and then continued our journey to Hemet, where we stayed at a hotel. Arriving in plenty of time before the evening activities started, our friends took us to a mall. We walked around the stores, and they stepped into a men's shop and insisted on buying Ralph a blazer. I was overwhelmed. I needed a better coat for the evening but had no idea I would be the recipient of one. What a gracious gift from these dear friends! As we walked around some more, Gail spotted a jewelry store and wanted to have her rings cleaned. The clerk said he would be happy to do this for her. When he finished her rings, they looked beautiful. He then offered to do Margie's. She told him she would like him to clean them but probably could not get them off her fingers. He told her that would be no problem. He went into the back room of the store and returned with a bottle of Windex. He sprayed her ring fingers, and immediately the rings came off. She was shocked! She has remembered this trick and used Windex many times since then, and it always works.

The anniversary event went off beautifully. It was such a blessing to see Dr. Amstutz, president of Shepherds, Al Pick, director of Church Ministries, and Dan DiDonato, Vice president for Development. What a tribute to God's abundant provision for a place like Shepherds! Margie and I are so grateful for the many years they cared for our precious daughter Joy.

Our travel home the next day was a blessed one. We seldom had the opportunity to travel with friends who are interested in Shepherds. We appreciated so much the Chehocks and their kindness in inviting us to join them for this special event. In addition, as you read above, that trip really "suited" me by making me the recipient of a beautiful blazer coat. God is so good. He knows our need and promises to supply. ***And my God shall supply all your need according to His riches in glory by Christ Jesus.*** (Philippians 4:19)

THE BALLOON THAT FAILED

---◆---

In our travels for Shepherds, we had many unique experiences. While in the Salton Sea area, people told us about an unusual place we should visit. We did, and the story is remarkable.

Years ago, Leonard Knight had tried many things after high school and was involved in several types of work. He was a born-again Christian, having received Jesus Christ as his personal Savior through his sister's influence. He had an inner compulsion to tell others of God's love. Eventually he painstakingly worked on a hot air balloon emblazoned with a huge sign, "God Loves You," or something similar. The balloon idea never worked, so he finally gave up on this project. He was in Niland, California, and with a half sack of cement he fashioned a small monument with his message of God's love on it. He kept adding to it, and it grew and grew.

SALVATION MOUNTAIN SIGN

This is how the Salvation Mountain began. This never-ending desire to make God's love known to people was the driving force behind Leonard's challenging work. It is fascinating to see how he accomplished this monumental task. At first, Leonard had to rummage in the garbage dump looking for paint. After people learned of his energetic goals, companies and individuals began bringing him paint. With objects from the dump and plenty of mud and sand, he could make this mountain secure and filled with reminders of God's goodness to humanity.

SALVATION MOUNTAIN

65

It is not easy to apply paint to dirt, but he developed a method that proved adequate, and with time he has accomplished what seemed to be an impossible task. One has to see this marvel of human determination to appreciate it. We walked up this mountain, around all the fascinating displays, and into cave-like museums. They were all secure with the ingenious system this man developed with God's help. He uses adobe blocks reinforced with straw to give stability to the structures. He also uses bales of straw to form rooms where he displays more of his creations.

Even though Leonard could have moved into one of these intriguing rooms he fashioned in his ***mountain,*** he chooses to live in the home he built on his truck, decorated much like Salvation Mountain. This man lives without any of the things we would call essential. No electricity, no fans, no air conditioning, no telephones, no running water or anything that we take for granted. He goes into town early in the morning, has a cup of coffee, and returns to spend the rest of the day on his favorite work, Salvation Mountain.

We wonder how many people he has influenced by this amazing demonstration of God's love for them. We can pray that all the visitors to this site will read the Scripture verses and be born again spiritually. ***And He said to them, Go into all the world and preach the gospel to every creature.*** (Mark 16:15) Leonard is doing this in his part of the world. Are you?

THE HIGHLIGHT OF THE YEAR

E ach year we looked forward to our trip to Union Grove, Wisconsin, to attend the Christmas-time festivities at Shepherds. Not only was it the unbelievable Christmas banquet for the employees, but a valuable time for the representatives to meet for fellowship and business. We had an added blessing also. Our daughter Joy was there, and we visited with her each day.

We profited during the meetings by hearing heart-warming reports from Dr. William Amstutz, the president, and several others, including Dan DeDonato. During our last year with Shepherds, the Shepherds College was beginning. It was a joy to attend some of the college classes and see the marvelous way these special young people were learning. They were taught valuable things to help them progress in their personal, spiritual, and social lives. We remember one day president Amstutz received a text message from the cooking instructor inviting us all for hot roast beef sandwiches with all the trimmings. They were delicious!

We representatives learned from each other as we shared meeting routines. It was such a treat to be together with others who were doing things we did, but in various places. It was a profitable time, and we learned much. The things we learned helped us be better Shepherds representatives to the churches. Part of being better representatives was learning the many facets of life at Shepherds. What a joy it was to visit with the clients and learn from them. Their stories inspired church congregations around America in a dynamic way.

The concluding banquet was a treat we will never forget. This was a gift to the employees and a delightful evening. Other invited guests made it a very inspirational time as we concluded our yearly visit to Shepherds.

We always left the campus with a nostalgic feeling one gets by being so close to an organization. They were so good to us by allowing Joy to live there for forty-five years. As we said our goodbyes to Joy and Shepherds, it was difficult. Margie and I relate to the Apostle Paul when he spoke these words long ago to the Philippian church he dearly loved: ***I thank my God upon every remembrance of you.*** (Philippians 1:3)

STRANGE TEMPERATURE CHANGE

———◆———

Traveling in the desert has its challenges. One week we were in northern Arizona, representing Shepherds to churches. From this area, we headed to California. Anyone who has traveled the desert knows how hot it can get. I drove a truck after high school graduation across the Arizona and California deserts and had many experiences with the heat.

Driving a truck pulling a 30 foot fifth-wheel trailer takes a lot of gas. Our route took us to Barstow, California, way out in the desert, where we had to stop for gas. Before filling up we found a rest stop and spent a few minutes there. The day before making this trip, the weather had been 110 degrees in the desert. We traveled many miles and noticed it was very cloudy. There was some wind blowing also, and we wondered what was happening. We pulled into a rest stop, not expecting what would come next. As soon as we opened the truck door, we felt a rush of cool air. Stepping out of the truck, we soon discovered we were in the middle of winter. It was the wrong month but so cold we had to put coats on. We could hardly believe it. After this shock, we found a gas station and filled the tanks before moving on. The station attendant said it was a remarkable change in weather in just a few short hours. That was a first for us, and we will never forget it.

We remember missionaries' stories of flights from their station to America at night when their children were sleeping.

MIRACLE MILES For God's Special People

Upon awaking in the morning, they were in a new country with different people, language, food, etc., and it was a difficult adjustment for them. Their children cried because they were afraid. We did not have that extreme reaction in the Mohave Desert, but it was COLD, and we never forgot the shock it was to our systems. Paul gives some good advice and personal testimony in these words: ***Not that I speak in regard to need, for I have learned in whatever state I am, to be content:*** (Philippians 4:11)

THEY TAUGHT US SO MUCH

B eing the parents of a child with developmental disabilities was a plus for us as we spoke to churches about
Shepherds. It was an honor to tell congregations about this
special place. Our daughter Joy taught us much that we will
never forget. Visiting Shepherds brought untold blessings,
because we could see our daughter and meet many others
in the home. Each one, with a unique personality, made our
visits to Shepherds very special.

The beautiful manner in which these residents accepted
each other was a tremendous blessing to us. No questioning
about a particular disability, no criticism for not being able to
verbalize, was only a "tip of the iceberg" to the great accep-
tance these precious people displayed. We soon learned that
we should never underestimate their amazing intelligence.
When we stepped on campus, they would come to us with
the exuberant statement, "You are Joy's mom and dad!" They
all seemed to know this. It would take us a long time to learn
their names, but they knew ours.

We watched them work, play, eat, and worship. We were
impressed with all they did. Their concern for one another
and their interpersonal relationships were amazing. Some we
met far exceeded our abilities, like the one who seemed to be
a perpetual calendar, knowing the exact day of my birth when
I gave her my birthdate. We found that some fellows were

sports experts, knowing the major players and the teams to which they belonged. In spiritual matters, we were impressed with their understanding of biblical truths and their memorization of Scripture verses.

In the work place, we saw them do routine jobs with great care and dedication. They did not seem to get bored with repetitious tasks as we do. What a gift! Some higher functional residents could do amazing things, putting objects in various categories. Some worked outside Shepherds and did well.

What an honor to have worked for and represented this wonderful home called Shepherds. We will never forget the lessons learned from God's special people, and we thank Him for calling us to represent them for a few years. How true this is: ***Know that the LORD, He is God; It is He who has made us, and not we ourselves; We are His people and the sheep of His pasture.*** (Psalm 100:3)

A SAFE PLACE

W e presented the ministry of Shepherds in a church where the folks were caring, loving, and generous. We had spoken there before, and the reception was always the best. The interchange of words at the conclusion of the service at the display table was always very important to us. My wife Margie seemed to evoke most of the conversations that took place. We felt that her being the mother of our Joy, who was developmentally disabled, was the reason they seemed to migrate to her end of table and visit. We were pleased with this.

We were careful about offerings for the ministry, even though it was because of them that the home could continue. Nevertheless, we always gave opportunities for folks to have a part in this vital work. Those interested in giving to Shepherds have many ways to do it. We displayed literature that outlined these. After the service this night, I noticed a confusion of some sort in the foyer of the church. Later, the person in charge told us that the very generous offering taken for Shepherds was missing almost immediately. Obviously, the thief, or thieves, knew exactly how to get the money. All were perplexed at how quickly it happened.

Later, the church purchased a floor safe, which was much better. Another blessing is that the church made up for the stolen money and gave Shepherds a very generous amount.

That was very gracious of them, and we thanked the Lord for His provision for this great ministry. The Apostle Paul reminded the Philippians of this when he penned this verse: **And my God shall supply all your need according to His riches in glory by Christ Jesus.** (Philippians 4:19)

TICK TALK

---◆---

In Polson, Montana, parked at the First Baptist Church, it happened. This church was our home base while we informed churches around the state about our Shepherds ministry. One afternoon in our fifth wheel trailer, Margie let out a loud "Oh no!" I wondered what had happened. She noticed a fine black mark on her hand that was itchy and slightly red. Because we have friends who have been plagued with the dreaded Lyme disease, she was afraid her worst nightmare had become a reality.

Fortunately, there was a drop-in clinic nearby, so I immediately took Margie there. In the meantime, before we got to the clinic, Margie had messed with this spot too much, and the black "thing" was no longer visible. The nurse tried to console Margie that she did not believe it was a tick or Lyme disease, but asked her to return later.

Because of Margie's numerous illnesses, she wanted to be on the safe side. We contacted her allergy specialist, and he sent her a kit with elaborate instructions how to get the proper procedure done. A specialized clinic in a distant city would do the test for Lyme disease. He also sent a prescription for medication she should begin taking immediately.

It was a not a good day for Margie. As if she did not have enough to occupy her mind with other things for which she was on medication, now she must add this to the list. Time went on, and eventually she learned that as far as medical science was concerned, she did not have Lyme disease. We thanked the Lord repeatedly for this, and I can assure you she took extra precautions where she walked while we were in Montana. We know that *Lyme disease* is the most common tick-borne illness in North America and Europe. This is the reason she was so concerned. We are very thankful for competent doctors and laboratories that can help those who need it from time to time. Margie and I are convinced of what Paul wrote in his epistle: ***Or do you not know that your body is the temple of the Holy Spirit who is in you, whom you have from God, and you are not your own?*** (1 Corinthians 6:19) Our desire is to take diligent care of our temple while down here doing God's work.

A SURPRISE AUDIENCE

———◆———

O ne of the benefits of traveling in the southland during the winter is the number of friends we met who traveled there to escape the frigid weather. We were in Tucson, Arizona, enjoying wonderful meetings and great weather. Our next stop was Mesa and Apache Junction. On the way to our destination that day, we stopped at The Old Country Buffet for a meal and then settled in at our next church, Calvary Baptist Church in Mesa. A dear friend, Al Hickinbotham from Ferndale, always presented us with a very generous gift certificate for this restaurant chain as we traveled. We deeply appreciated his kindness.

Our friends Glen and Gerry Thomason were nearby at the Road Haven facility. They had secured a place there from a friend and were housesitting. Apparently, this was a customary practice with those who frequent such retirement centers. They took us to a swap meet, where we walked through four very large longhouses. That was a challenge for Margie, but she made it okay. It was also very interesting to see the enormity of this place and the unbelievable amount of things offered for sale. It was amazing to say the least. Later, visiting with the Thomasons, they asked if we would be willing to do our Shepherds presentation for the members of their organization. We said we would be happy to do this, and a time was set. We had only done this in churches, so this was a new experience. We arrived early and set up our equipment and literature table. Then we waited for our guests to arrive. They did, and we had a very good group of seniors with whom we shared the wonderful story of Shepherds. Most had never heard about this home. It was thrilling to see the reaction of these seasoned adults to the ministry of Shepherds. Many had loved ones who would definitely benefit from such a place. It was a privilege for Margie and me to talk with so many at the conclusion of the service. There was a real interest in what we said, and we always prayed that those attending would take the literature and later be led to donate to this ministry. It was an unusual audience, because they were from so many different places and represented a variety of denominations. They were touched by the presentation, and we always thanked the Lord for the privilege of showing them about Shepherds. Although our situation was completely different from that of Peter and John, the answer of these two men is what we felt as we stood to represent Shepherds no matter where we were: ***For we cannot but speak the things which we have seen and heard.*** (Acts 4:20)

AN APPETITE FOR BRAZILIAN FOOD

I t is interesting how former missionaries have flashbacks of things that happened on the field years ago. We were in the Seattle, Washington, area having a meeting for Shepherds. On the way home, we remembered we had heard about a store in the area that sold Brazilian food. We looked a long time and finally found it. It was amazing! As we walked into this store, we got the same feeling we used to experience in the stores in Brazil.

We recognized many Brazilian food items on the shelves. In the back of the store, around tables, were Brazilians speaking their beautiful language, Portuguese. It was delightful to see the sights and smell the familiar odors we used to in Brazil.

We chose a couple of items and headed to the cashier. We spoke Portuguese to the cashier, and perhaps they were surprised we spoke their language. It was fun, and we were happy to have found a place like this. Later, we discovered a bigger and better store in the Seattle area. They had a larger stock of Brazilian canned goods and other items.

At this larger store, we discovered they had a web site that offered every item we saw in the store. We were excited, went online, and ordered some things. We had them shipped to us. A few years ago, the miracle of doing this was free shipping. We could hardly believe it. Now there is a price, so we seldom order our favorite items via the Internet. You would think there never would be a desire for things we found on the mission field, but some things you like are not usually sold in America. We remember the children of Israel when they longed for the things of Egypt. ***We remember the fish which we ate freely in Egypt, the cucumbers, the melons, the leeks, the onions, and the garlic;*** (Numbers 11:5) It was certainly different than our story. They wanted to leave God's place for them and return to the slavery of Egypt. Thank God, the Brazilian food is wonderful, and we would return if we could preach the gospel again to those dear people.

TO KEEP IN FOCUS

The big question: Which luxuries do you want to take with you in the trailer? Some things are not luxuries, others are. When we started, I did not consult with anyone about this, but I decided that one thing that is supposedly a luxury was going with us. That luxury was our DirecTV. How to operate this on the road remained a mystery, but as we went along, we learned. I bought plenty of TV cable with the right fittings to extend it if needed. I also looked at RV catalogs and finally decided on the right tripod on which to mount the satellite dish. This dish was portable and easy for travel.

The DirecTV receiver is about the size of old video recorder/players. One aspect of DirecTV viewing is getting the receiver focused in the right direction so it will work. I asked questions and bought a special compass to focus the unit correctly to receive the satellite signal. Arriving at our destination, I would first mount the satellite dish on the tripod, which was securely stationed and not wobbly. Then I connected the cable to the dish and the other end to the receiver. Now I was ready to focus. Turning on the receiver and entering either the nearest city or the zip code would give the proper pitch and angle of the dish. With that information, I would first set the angle of the dish according to specifications. This would point it in the general direction of that satellite in the sky.

With those adjustments, I attached another machine pur-chased at an RV place, which was an in-line meter from the dish to the receiver. It gave an audible and visual signal. When I rotated the dish according to the reading on the compass, the needle on the inbox signal detector would swing to the highest point to the right when I was focused on the satel-lite. It would also emit a high frequency audible sound. Many times this would happen within minutes after setting up. At other times it took a long time to find the right satellite. There are many up there, and sometimes the meter would indicate a focus, but there was no picture reaching the monitor on our TV. We would have to keep trying until we hit the right one. What a joy it was when that happened!

In forested areas, the process was very difficult. I have spent as much as four hours trying to get the satellite focused through a distant hole in the treetops. What a break it was when a picture finally appeared on the monitor. Yes, this was a luxury, but getting the daily news and some other pro-grams was such a blessing. We enjoyed some Christian pro-grams, too. In some areas where we parked, the wind blew so hard that it knocked the tripod over. I discovered I could hang three one-gallon milk containers filled with water on the tripod and it would stay stationary. Toward the end of our travels, the DirecTV changed. If we had continued, things would have been quite different.

Even though it was enjoyable having this service no matter where we were, how much better it is that God takes care of our needs and us. That is much more important than a televi-sion system out in the desert. ***Every good gift and every per-fect gift is from above, and comes down from the Father of lights, with whom there is no variation or shadow of turning.*** (James 1:17)

SHE HAS DONE WHAT SHE COULD

In every church we visited while representing Shepherds, I taught something from the Bible that would challenge the church members to do what they could for the Lord. We think the Shepherds residents are the best examples of this. Margie and I were impressed with the Christian service the residents performed in churches. It was a blessing to learn all we could about the residents and what they did for the Lord.

Many times, I used Mark 14:1-9 and told the story of the woman who anointed the head of Jesus, and the criticism which followed. Then I explained in detail about the flask of ointment (perfume). My friend years ago in Phoenix who was a geologist, told me interesting things about his discoveries in the Holy Land. He explained how the flask was useless once it had been broken to pour out the perfume. The punch line of this message was when Jesus told the disciples, "Let her alone. Why do you trouble her? She has done a good work for Me.... *She has done what she could*." Her life, like the perfume, had been poured out in service to Him.

Using this phrase from Jesus, I spoke of Shepherds residents, whom most people thought could do very little for Jesus. However, as we observed, they were doing a great service ministering in churches. Those who remember Dr. Andrew Wood, the first Director of Shepherds, will never forget the amazing influence the boys who travelled with him had on churches. Dr. Wood interviewed them, and they would answer his Bible questions and quote many memorized Scripture verses. Their solos and personal testimonies were always a blessing. In our years with Shepherds, that ministry continued as Mr. Pick and others took residents with them to minister in churches. When one young man sang, *It will be worth it all when we see Jesus,* there was usually not a dry eye in the church. I wonder how many of us could be included in Jesus' statement; **she has done what she could.** (Mark 14:8)

A NOSTALGIC VISIT

In our ministry for Shepherds, we eventually came to Phoenix, Arizona, my hometown since I was 5 years old. After we settled at our host church, we decided to do some sight-seeing around town. Things had changed through the years, and most of the old landmarks were gone. We really had to search to find anything that even looked familiar.

We first found Thirty-Eighth Street and drove down it, carefully trying to identify anything that would remind us of where I lived as a youth. Finally, we saw a house set back from the road with a large front lawn, and I determined this was our old home. It really had not changed too much, except the barn at the rear of the house was gone. It was there my Dad had raised goats. Goat milk is special, and many folks purchased it for their children who were intolerant to cow's milk. Next, we tried to find my brother Harold's house. We found it on Piccadilly Road, and of course, it brought back many memories. It was in this house that Margie and I knelt beside our daughter Joy's bed and gave her and her life to the Lord. This was a LONG time before we knew anything about Shepherds, where she eventually lived for over 45 years.

Our next search took us to Thirty-Seventh Street looking for Grandpa and Grandma Robin's old house. With some difficulty, we finally found it. Grandpa called it the Robin's Nest. When grandpa died, I lived in this house until the Lord called me to Biola Bible College, because I did not want Grandma to live alone. Grandpa was a master carpenter, having built their home and some of the lush hotels years ago in Miami, Florida.

We still had another house to find. My brother Harold traded his house on Twenty-Fourth Place for the one my folks used to occupy on Piccadilly. Therefore, it was in this house my folks lived many years, prior to coming to Ferndale, Washington. When Margie and I returned from Brazil, we felt it best for them to be with us in their sunset years. We found the Twenty-Fourth Place house, and memories flashed through my mind of all the things that had happened there. It was in this house, while visiting them during our furlough from Brazil, that I noticed a slight tremor in Mother's hand. She told us she suffered from Parkinson's disease. We never knew any person who handled this problem better than she did. She was a real spiritual giant and lived what she believed. She was always a tremendous example to us.

Something happened to us while photographing the house from the opposite side of the street. A man and his son stepped out of their house and walked toward us. I told them I took the picture because my parents lived in the house years ago. I secretly felt they were going to be unhappy with me. On the contrary, the man's wife joined him, and we had a pleasant conversation. I told them that when my folks left this house and went to Ferndale, they gave my brother the house. The couple asked our name, and when I said "Poulson", she said that name was on the papers when they purchased it. What a small world! Moses told the children of Israel something that reminded me of our experience looking for these old residences: ***Remember the days of old, Consider the years of many generations. Ask your father, and he will show you; Your elders, and they will tell you:*** (Deuteronomy 32:7)

A SCARY RIDE OVER AN OLD MOUNTAIN ROAD

This may be an unfair way to introduce you to our first trip to Glacier National Park. Because we were so close to this famous landmark, we decided to take a day to explore. It did not take us long to get to the entrance, and soon we were on our way up this amazing mountain range. As the road started its more severe incline upward, we could not help but notice the grandeur of the scenery.

CONTINENTAL DIVIDE– MONTANA

Before long, we were on a road over the precarious moun-tain range labeled "Going-to-the-Sun Road." According to the brochure we secured as we entered the park, it was 53 miles long and completed in 1932. Also known simply as the Sun Road, it bisects the park and is the only route that ventures deep into the park. It goes over the Continental Divide at Logan Pass, 6,646 feet high at the midpoint. Our Ford 250 with its side mirrors was a challenge to drive. For Margie it was more than that. When we were on a stretch of the road where she was on the "outside" edge, looking down, it was not fun at all. It was scary. Because the road was so old, it was also much narrower than modern roads. At times, we had to be creative as we passed other vehicles. One time I remember having to "hug" the mountain to make room for a passing car. In this maneuver, the right side mirror had to swing back against the truck door.

Finally, we made it to the top of the pass. There was a building there with information about the area, some restrooms, and an opportunity to buy a snack. In walking around, we took a trail downward and soon encountered a famous mountain goat. They are large and imposing as they stare at you with those penetrating eyes and huge horns. We definitely wanted to stay on their good side, as the saying goes. Glacier National Park offers so much that you cannot comment on everything. There just is not time. However, we were intrigued with the *triple divide.* Glacier's Triple Divide Peak (8020 ft. /2446 m) is a rather rare hydrologic feature. From the summit, water flows to the *Atlantic Ocean*, the *Pacific Ocean*, and *Hudson Bay*. You can see the peak from the Going-to-the-Sun Road in the Two Dog Flats area, on the east side of the park.

Instead of continuing on the highway over to the east side of Glacier National Park, we retraced our route, returning the same way. The pictures we took tell the magnificent story of God's unique handiwork. We were in awe as we witnessed this marvel of creation. In addition, to think our loving Lord did all this when He first spoke things into existence is miraculous! I am so thankful we have a God who did this and in whom we can entrust our lives. ***By faith we understand that the worlds were framed by the word of God, so that the things which are seen were not made of things which are visible.*** (Hebrews 11:3)

A SMALL CHURCH WITH A BIG HEART

M ontana, Big Sky Country, and we love it! When we realized we were going to have the privilege of representing Shepherds in Montana, we were very happy. It was all new to us as we traveled in this great state. After a few meetings, we ventured out into more distant places.

SWAN VALLEY BAPTST CHURCH—MONTANA

From our spot at Lake Blaine, we drove without the trailer to Swan Lake, about seventy-five miles away. Driving early in the morning, motorists are extra cautious, as deer roam freely and are numerous in Montana. There were many, and we had to be alert while driving. Arriving at the church early, we introduced ourselves to Pastor Charles Wood, who greeted us with a smile and a great Montana handshake.

Soon we started setting up our things in the very small auditorium. Our display table was at the front, and we got our projector set up in the aisle. Everything about this church was great, except for one thing. It was a very small building, like a miniature church. The community is small, so their building was ample for the number of people that attended. A loving pastor and wife, incredible children, and church members who were warm and friendly were what made this place so special. When believers meet, we are friends immediately, and the fellowship we experienced in this church was outstanding. The church was very receptive to the Shepherds message. I do not know if anyone had ever been there before to talk about Shepherds, but these folks knew much about the ministry and had supported it for years.

After the evening service, they took a very generous offering, which humbled us. The generous gift for Shepherds that day demonstrated the godly leadership by Pastor Wood. Pastor Wood has worked at a secular job all the years he has been pastor there. He works very hard at a sawmill, but with smiling face and a heart for God and people, he directs this work with joy. We were impressed.

After the morning service, we were guests at the pastor's home for lunch. What a delicious meal his wife Elizabeth served us! We enjoyed them both, plus their fine children. We left this little church with great respect for this pastor and his flock. The offering, which was larger than that of most churches twice its size, impressed us greatly. In fact, just a short time after our being there, their yearly Shepherds Sunday was approaching, and Pastor Wood definitely told me they would be sending a very generous offering to Shepherds at that time. What can we say? Such dedication from a small group of people in a small church was a powerful lesson to us. I forgot to say that the church is beautiful on the outside also. Inside, I imagine you could walk from the entrance to the wall behind the pulpit in a matter of seconds. However, the HEART of this church is big, and we praise God for what we learned on that trip to Swan Valley Baptist Church. Like us, Paul was not seeking a gift from the Philippians, but he knew they were generous and that God was giving them spiritual fruit for their giving hearts: ***Not that I seek the gift, but I seek the fruit that abounds to your account.*** (Philippians 4:17) This Montana church has been a blessing to Shepherds.

TOO FAR AWAY FOR HELP

O ccasionally when we worked for Shepherds, our schedules permitted us to fulfill some extra meetings to which
we had previously committed. This time it was north of Boise,
Idaho, at a place called Warm Lake. And it was warm. We
walked to the water's edge and could see steam coming out
of the leaves and debris, which really surprised us. We had
been to this camp before to minister to senior saints from
some churches in that part of Idaho.

I was scheduled to give Bible lessons several times. Those
who know my method at these settings will remember I
also gave a series of lessons in God's Handiwork in Nature.
I concluded long ago that some liked these better than the
Bible lessons.

One afternoon they asked me to speak about our ministry
with Shepherds, which I always enjoyed doing. I got everything
ready early, and it was a good thing I did, because as I was
setting up we had a problem almost immediately. I had the
projector turned on and was beginning to go through a practice run with the slides. Suddenly, the projector lamp burned
out. Seldom in our years as representatives for Shepherds
had that ever happened, but this day it did. The first rule for
missionaries is to carry an extra bulb. Therefore, I immediately removed the burned-out bulb and replaced it with the
new one. Then the fun began. To my utter amazement, when

I flipped on the machine, this bulb also burned out. Now I had no bulb and we were 200 miles round trip from a place where we could possibly find one. I knew we didn't have time to do this. We learned years ago on the mission field to try to be resourceful in all situations, but I wondered what I could do to show these slides. Warm Lake Baptist Camp had an overhead projector that worked, but that bulb would not work in the slide projector. My mental wheels were turning fast. I removed the bulb assembly from the overhead projector, and with the wires still connected, tried to make it fit in the precise place of the slide projector. That would help project the slide onto the screen. I worked, twisted, relocated, and experimented with so many options that it almost made me dizzy.

Finally, in a wonderful answer to prayer, it worked. By holding the lamp a certain way, it projected well onto the screen. It was awkward, but both machines needed to be on for the process to work. I was so thankful to the Lord that the slide show went off without too much difficultly. I admit it was really a hot job managing both machines and especially holding the base of the overhead projector lamp so it would not burn me. The camp director was amazed how I did what I did. We gave all the credit to the Lord, who gave me wisdom to make these adaptations. The Lord's appeal through David has meant much to me. ***Call upon Me in the day of trouble; I will deliver you, and you shall glorify Me.*** (Psalm 50:15)

TOO HOT FOR COMFORT

Traveling brings many experiences. We learned this when we were in southern states during the summer. I was used to hot weather, because I had lived in Phoenix, Arizona, but Margie was more accustomed to cooler climates like those that she had in Ferndale, Washington.

Going over mountain passes in the summer was a challenge to those who like to be comfortable. When the outside temperature is hot, there are signs posted periodically advising drivers to turn off their air conditioner units in their cars or trucks. These units can cause a car's motor to overheat and do considerable damage. Therefore, for safety reasons, we opened the windows in our truck, turned off the air conditioner, and let the warm air rush into the truck. When air is in motion from a fan, it is usually better than driving with the windows shut. If the mountain grades were not too steep, I would have the air conditioner on but watch the heat gauge to see if the motor was cool enough.

It was a very hot day when we pulled into Brawley, California. The pastor showed us where we could hook up and get electricity for our fifth wheel. I got the fifth wheel set up and stepped inside the trailer to see if the temperature had moderated a bit since turning on the units. A glance at the thermometer told the story. Inside, the temperature was 102, and outside it was 118 degrees. Therefore, it was better inside than out, but still very HOT! We normally used evaporative coolers because Margie did much better with them. That day we had the air conditioners going, and I filled the evaporative coolers with water and turned them on. By nighttime, it was tolerable inside, and we were grateful for electricity that made it all possible. **"And when you see the south wind blow, you say, *'There will be hot weather'; and there is."*** (Luke 12:55)

AAA TO THE RESCUE

Y ou learn quickly about insurance companies. It is easy to think nothing will ever happen to you, but this is folly. When you least expect it, you might need help. I have written about the times AAA or Good Sam came to our rescue along the road or in towns when we needed them.

Here is one we have not mentioned before. We were doing our weekly laundry at a laundromat in Pasco, Washington. In between loads, Margie had walked down the strip mall to a grocery store while I kept an eye on the machines. We went through a routine on washdays, so things went well. We finished and started to put things into the truck, first into the back bed of the truck and next inside. However, wait a minute. Where are my keys? I do not have them! What a horrible feeling! Margie did not have her keys, because they were in her purse inside the truck.

There was only one thing to do, call AAA. That number is right on your ID card, and so in a second I was talking to the dispatcher. After getting our AAA number, they wanted to know our location. Ordinarily they give an estimate of how long it will take to arrive on the scene. They did, and it would take about 45 minutes. So now we had to wait. AAA arrived a little sooner than projected. It was nice to have this very kind man, with the proper tool, like the thieves use, get your truck door open in a moment. After signing my name and "thanks," he was on his way, and so were we. Who would ever think we would use this verse for a locksmith, but here it is: ***Call upon Me in the day of trouble; I will deliver you, and you shall glorify Me.*** (Psalm 50:15)

TWO TRUCKS WE NEVER
DREAMED OF OWNING

FORD 150, 250 AND 350

As "greenhorns", we set out to do things we had never done before. We realized that to be effective in our ministry for Shepherds, we had to have a semblance of privacy as we traveled around the eight western states. A Ford 150 towed our first trailer, a fifth wheel. These trucks are very good for pulling a trailer. In my great inexperience, however, we purchased a singlewide trailer. In other words, no slide-outs, or tip-outs, which give more room. We soon learned that it was not sufficient to live extended periods of time in such confined areas within this trailer. Therefore, we graduated to one that had a push-out in the living room and bedroom. Our truck was too small to pull a heavy fifth wheel. Through a providential and extremely gracious gift from my brother Ernie, in Singapore, we purchased a used Ford 250. A car salesperson, a friend of ours, recommended it, and my brother provided the finances. What a blessing that vehicle was! We will always be grateful to Ernie and Verda Poulson for this wonderful truck. We travelled thousands of miles in it and never had any major mechanical problems. What a blessing!

Incredibly, as time went on, we discovered a used trailer that was better than the previously new one we had purchased. A good friend of ours, Armond Daws, lost his wife, Helen, and did not travel anymore, and so he sold us his four-door Ford 350. You might wonder why we needed a Ford 350. The fact that this truck had four doors revolutionized our ministry in a wonderful way. Previously when we ended our ministry on Sundays we had to juggle all our equipment into two compartments mounted on the truck bed. We put the rest behind the driver and passenger seats. It was awkward to say the least, but we did this for a long time. When we had the trailer already hooked to the vehicle, it was almost impossible to access these exterior storage units.

With the Ford 350, we no longer had this problem. What a blessing to quickly put the equipment in the truck! It also enabled us to transport more than just the two of us. One time friends from Anchorage met us, and we could take them in our truck to a local restaurant for a meal and fellowship. It was a nostalgic day when we parted with each truck. We always rejoiced and thanked the Lord for His gracious provision by my brother Ernie and Armond Daws. It was truly amazing how God supplied just the right truck and fifth wheel we needed. Paul's words proved to be the answer for us, and we praise the Lord. ***And my God shall supply all your need according to His riches in glory by Christ Jesus.*** (Philippians 4:19)

UNDER LOCK AND KEY

I t is easy to forget we live in days that can bring challenges that we did not expect nor want. We have never been accustomed to leaving our truck or trailer unlocked while we were gone. We know people who still do not lock their cars in our own country, but we prefer locking ours.

HOW WE USED OUR GENERATOR

Whenever we found it necessary to start up our little Honda generator, we were concerned that someone could just pick it up and carry it away. That is true because it was lightweight and easy to carry. I went into a hardware company in Clovis, California, and explained to the clerk what I wanted. Surprisingly, he told me that just before me, a man had come for the same thing. His generator was on his truck in the parking lot. After purchasing a chain, he returned to the truck and the generator was gone. We did not want that to happen to us.

With a heavy chain and a very robust padlock, I fastened the Honda to one of the trailer's stabilizer jacks. It was secure and now theft proof. We could sleep much better after that. Yes, the Honda noise was equivalent to that of two men talking normally. What a blessing!

Again, we encountered a possible problem when people started looking at our satellite dish receiver. Normally it was right next to the trailer, so I got a lighter chain and a good lock, thus securing it to the trailer. Therefore, with the door locked, and the generator and satellite dish secure, we could sleep in peace.

It seems that about everything comes with locks. We know that even a lock is only a temporary security when a thief is around the corner, as they are experts at breaking in. Jesus warned us about our worldly possessions. *But lay up for yourselves treasures in heaven, where neither moth nor rust destroys and where thieves do not break in and steal*. (Matthew 6:20)

EVAPORATIVE COOLERS

E vaporative coolers work best in hot, dry climates. .
On one of our trips into California, the evaporative cooler in our bedroom gave out, and we looked for a new one. That started a series of buying and returning we had never done before. I would put one in the bedroom and find it did not fit the space, or it just did not seem to cool as it should. I think I tried four different machines before finding one that worked. I was amazed that the stores would allow us to return the units with no questions. One time I used the Internet to find one we wanted. We found one in stock in a town about thirty-five miles away. I put a hold on it, and we drove there and bought it. That night we were very glad to have the cool breeze filling our bedroom so we could sleep. Evaporative coolers take a lot of water. I never did measure how much we used in each 24-hour period, but it was many gallons. The pay-off is the economy of these units. They use about as much energy as a 150-watt light bulb compared to the astronomical amount of electricity an air conditioner takes. Most church plug-ins could not handle the extra amperes needed to run air conditioner units. Therefore, we were grateful for this very practical way to keep cool in hot weather. When it is hot and you are uncomfortable, it is easy to complain. Paul reminds us of this, in Philippians 2:14: ***Do all things without complaining and disputing.***

A PLACE TO PARK OUR TRAILER

N ormally we would park our trailer in a different town and location every seven days. It was not always this way, because in some locations we could leave the trailer and travel on Sunday to a city just driving our truck. We enjoyed it this way.

The Baptist church in Forest Ranch, California, scheduled us for meetings. This small town had a very lovely church. The Forest Ranch Baptist Church gave us opportunity to present the Shepherds Ministries, which we greatly appreciated. Arriving in this town, we called the pastor, who directed us to Bob and Ina Moody, our hosts for the weekend. A few miles on up the road from the church, in the beautiful mountains, there were tall pine trees, and there was our spot to park the trailer. The Moodys lived in a home they had purchased on the edge of an immense valley. From their home, one could see miles down the valley to the lowlands in the distance. Their home was fascinating. It was large, with many rooms on several floors. We were impressed beyond words when first seeing the house. It appeared that the chimney alone was about four floors high. We had never seen anything like it. The décor of the house was spectacular, and the floor was made of slabs of special stone. All was impressive, to say the least. Mr. Moody had planned wisely, and with an astute understanding of real estate, he had purchased this site at the right time.

Along with the beautiful house came much land. On this, he had a vision for a home for missionaries to use while on furlough. Missionaries from Brazil were living in this guesthouse when we arrived there. We, too, were from Brazil, so we had much in common with this family. Another service for missionaries and itinerants was a very well designed RV park. This is where we parked our trailer while in the area. This location was a few miles from the church over a dirt road that led out to the main highway. It took about twenty minutes to get to the church. The RV park came fully equipped with electricity, water, and dumpsites at each location. What a break and treat this was for us! Many times, if we stayed more than a week in a place, we had to find a dumpsite before moving on to the next place.

We thoroughly enjoyed fellowship in the church. They were most gracious to us when we spoke about Shepherds. We were always impressed how the ministry of this wonderful Home touched people. It was an honor for us to represent Shepherds in the churches. The friendships made during these visits were amazing. To this day, we have friendships and people email us from some of these contacts.

One special men's breakfast I will never forget. The men gathered for fellowship and a nice breakfast. The morning I was there, I figured the cook was a joker and probably testing this former missionary and pastor. I was not the only recipient of the episode, I am sure. When I took my first bite of pancake, I immediately sensed an unusual amount of roughage. For a moment, i was perplexed, not knowing how I should react. However, when I discovered pine needles laced throughout the pancake, I knew this was some kind of joke. Finally, the men came to my rescue and admitted this was a practical joke. We all had a hearty laugh over this and continued with the meal and fellowship.

We stayed a little longer at this special site on the mountain, helping the Moodys with some tasks around their place. We were also guests at their home for a delicious meal prepared by Mrs. Moody. We had an opportunity to revisit this church and repeat the blessings, minus the prank breakfast. We will always appreciate the hospitality shown us; also Pastor Chip Ross for his kindness in having us come to his church. At this church, we saw Paul's admonition come true: ***Distributing to the needs of the saints, given to hospitality.*** (Romans 12:13)

UNEXPECTED ANGELS

Sometimes during Christmas, we would leave our fifth wheel trailer parked at a church and drive the truck back to Ferndale, our home. One year we did this and came home to spend the vacation with our family. We thoroughly enjoyed these times, even though the trip was often long and adventurous.

RAWLIE POULSON FAMILY

We had a wonderful time with family, and now it was time to leave and resume our scheduled meetings for Shepherds in California. As often happens, it was a snowy trip, and the Siskiyou mountain range presented us with a challenge unlike any other.

As we made our ascent on Interstate 5, we noticed cars slowing down. The snow was light, but everything was snow-covered. Then the brilliant yellow alert signs warned us that all vehicles had to stop and chain up. This was not a cheery announcement for us because of the tremendous inconvenience of putting chains on our truck. I knew how to do it. Ever since my double knee replacement surgery, I have been careful not to put too much weight on my knees. I carried a small stool to help me in the process. As we turned into the designated area to start the arduous project, a kind man and his daughter approached, asking if we had chains. I assured him we did and gave him a short story about my knees. He could look and see we were senior citizens. Without a moment's hesitation, he kindly explained that he and his daughter would be happy to put them on for us.

You cannot imagine the joy of seeing these complete strangers dive in and install the chains in no time. We thanked them profusely and offered to pay them for their service. They accepted our gratitude but did not want any reimbursement for what they did. To enhance the extraordinary kindness of this couple, what followed utterly amazed us. The man motioned for us to follow him up and over the mountain. This we gladly did, as the snow was increasing and it was easier to follow a car immediately in front of us. Mile after mile passed, and over the summit there was another designated place for motorists to remove their chains. This kind man and his daughter waved us over to this spot and without a word, removed the chains, put them in the truck, and kindly wished us a nice trip.

Have you ever heard of such? We will never forget this act of kindness. Immediately we thought what the Bible says about angels. ***Do not forget to entertain strangers, for by so doing some have unwittingly entertained angels.*** (Hebrews 13:2) That happened to us on that trip.

UNIVERSAL DRUG STORE

―――――◆―――――

W hen I accepted the position as representative for Shepherds on the West Coast, we had to learn how to get Margie's medications.

At first, we thought it would be possible for someone to mail the needed prescriptions to us, but we soon discovered that was too difficult. We had to find another way to get our prescriptions. I guess through trial and error, we learned a lot. Because we were members of Costco, we investigated the possibility of receiving the needed medications via their many stores around the country. We spent a good deal of time with doctor offices, and finally worked out a solution. Then we had to put it into practice to see if it would work. We began with our physician, who phoned a prescription to Costco in Bellingham, Washington. In turn, we called the pharmacy department and gave them information about where we would be on a certain day. Along with that, we had to give the number of the Costco store, its location, and the contact number for telephone communication.

Arriving in a certain city, we called the local Costco and told them the Bellingham, Washington, Costco would be sending them the prescription. We then checked with the MEDICINE ON THE GO where we were, to see if it had arrived. If It had, we went and picked it up. This was an amazing way to get Margie's medication. I believe it worked without too many glitches along the way, and we were thankful.

Coupled with the Costco method, we had another with Group Health Cooperative, our health insurance provider. We had started with them years before our ministry with Shepherds. They have an automated system or direct line to a staff person who would take our order and process it. Almost all medications we ordered via Group Health Cooperative came in frozen packs. It was amazing that when we opened it, the ice pack always had plenty of "cold" still in it. What a wonderful way God took care of us on the road! We have come a long way since the days of the Apostle Paul when he wanted things as he traveled and requested that Timothy bring them. ***Bring the cloak that I left with Carpus at Troas when you come--and the books, especially the parchments.*** (2Timothy 4:13) Thank God for a postal system and Costco that served us well.

SCHEDULING MEETINGS

Each Shepherds representative was responsible for scheduling meetings in churches in his assigned area. Fortunately, Mr. Alan Pick, Director of Church Relations at Shepherds, was our source for all questions related to this subject. Mr. Pick set the example by demonstrating how one needs to be persistent and patient in securing meetings to inform churches about Shepherds Home.

Not only did he show us how to get meetings; he also met with us when we were on campus at Shepherds, and we jointly discussed different themes and messages for such occasions. We combined our ideas and were encouraged to use these in churches we visited. Scheduling is an art that takes time to develop and that one never feels he has achieved. With a calendar in hand, hours of phone work are necessary to fill in the dates. We avoided important holidays and times of the year when churches have special programs. We learned early on to be patient and not get discouraged when scheduling seemed very slow. It would not be abnormal to dial a number for a month or more without any answer. When churches returned our calls, we considered it a victory, and we thanked the Lord for each one.

Dr.Andrew and Betty (deceased) Wood

We discovered that a representative had not visited in our area of the U.S.A. for a very long time. Dr. Wood, founder and first Director of Shepherds, had traveled much in these states, as we discovered upon arrival in many churches. They told us we were the first ones to visit them since Dr. Wood and the boys were in their churches. This was a hard act to follow. However, our presentation was very personal, as our daughter Joy was a resident there. The churches were happy, and we were happy to be able to tell folks about this wonderful home. It was obvious that some did not know about Shepherds, but in all our years with this ministry we seldom found those who did not want us for a meeting.

Mr. Pick set a good example by working diligently on his appointments. He told me it was his goal to have most slots filled, if possible, by the end of May. Anyone who waited too long after Christmas to start their calling could end up with many open dates. What a thrill it was to have this major task under control. In working with pastors, we realized they had busy schedules. We were thankful when we could talk with them and schedule meetings. I think of the apostle Paul when he gave guidelines for conducting a church, giving this wholesome advice. The same applied to us as we scheduled meetings. ***Let all things be done decently and in order.*** (1Corinthians 14:40)

WATER ON THE WRONG SIDE

———◆———

High winds and RV's do not mix well. We witnessed an amazing sight following a rig in southern California one time. The wind came suddenly and was so strong that the window in the fifth wheel trailer in front of us blew out of its casing. That is a strong wind. Usually there were warning advisories about such things. Occasionally, however, they come without previous warning.

Our southbound trip on Interstate 5 from Bellingham, Washington, was going well. We made it through the famous Siskiyou mountain range in Oregon and into the other mountainous region prior to entering Redding, California. The rains were fierce. Our new 28 foot Cougar fifth wheel pulled exceptionally well through the winds and rain.

Our destination on that trip was El Centro, California. After the heavy rains of northern California, we passed Bakersfield, California, and took highway 58 east. Then we went south to get on a main route eastward, from which we went further south to El Centro. All had gone well on that trip, and we were happy to reach El Centro. It was good to see our good friends Pastor and Mrs. Albert Sanchez.

At their home, where we always parked our rig, we started setting up as we had done many times before. Once the trailer was in the right place, I opened the *slide-out* or *pop out*. This slide-out extends the interior of the trailer to a larger size and is very nice. The slide-out is very heavy, probably weighing as much as 600 pounds. The wonderfully geared motor does it with the greatest of ease and is much better than in past days when it had to be cranked by hand.

As the slide-out extends to its maximum point, the inside rug in what is called the social area of the trailer--the dining room, kitchen, and living room-- becomes larger. All this is in a relatively small space, but it looks very spacious when the slide-out is open. We noticed the beautiful new rug now exposed was completely soaked. What a sad way to start out with our new Cougar trailer! The driving rains of northern California had entered the RV, and it was all wet. What a disappointment!

The only thing going for us was the heat of the El Centro valley. It was very HOT! Our pastor friend, Albert Sanchez, helped by placing high velocity fans focused on the wet rugs. The hot weather from outside and now the pressure cooker heat on the inside with the aid of fan air got them well dried by the next day.

The next time we were home we took the trailer back to the dealer, and for several hundred dollars, a dam was installed at a crucial point where the slide-out moves in and out of the main body of the trailer. We often wondered why that dam was not part of the original manufacturer's package. That would eliminate headaches and disappointments for many, we are sure. For this reason, we did not keep that unit very long. We traded it in for one much nicer and more practical.

The Lord sovereignly sends the rain, and He is the One who causes it all to happen. We do not question that, as this wonderful verse explains: *He causes the vapors to ascend from the ends of the earth; He makes lightning for the rain; He brings the wind out of His treasuries.* (Psalm 135:7) We were just curious as to why dealers who sell these machines do not make them ready for rains BEFORE they sell them instead of AFTERWARD.

WE ALWAYS PARKED THERE

---◆---

We spent many wonderful weeks at Faith Baptist Church in Stockton, California. Each time we planned a trip for Shepherds, we tried to make it our midway point. From this spot, we moved out on weekends to different churches in the Bay Area and elsewhere. The church was very accommodating. We enjoyed fellowshipping with the folks during the week and anytime we did not have a meeting scheduled.

In early afternoon, we arrived at the church and pulled our truck and trailer alongside the Sunday School building, which was closest to the main road in front of the church. Just past this building, we went out into an open field covered with nice green grass. We stayed close to the Sunday School building and headed straight back toward the backside of this lot. Before getting there, we made a sharp left turn. This positioned the rig so we could back into the designated spot underneath the shade of some large trees. However, as we started backing into the lot, we were only a few feet onto the field when I noticed that things were slipping. The lush green grass and moist dirt in which it was growing did not provide enough traction for our rig. In an instant, we were stuck and unable to move.

Thankfully, we had good road insurance from two companies. We used the one we thought was best qualified for our predicament. I called Good Sam, and within an hour they were there with their rig to start the recovery process. A job that we calculated would take minutes turned out to be an enormous task for Mr. Good Sam. After four hours of tedious work, he was finally able to get our unit mobile again. We did not try that spot again. The front entrance of the church was a large cement area. We chose a spot close to the church but backed it in so we would not take so many parking spaces. It worked out well, and we were grateful to have a good place to park.

On previous visits to this church, we had always parked near the place we were stuck, as the field was dry grass. However, this time it was a different time of the year and things were still green and growing. Therefore, even though we had parked there many times, this was not the right time. We learned a good lesson that day. We returned there many times through the years and enjoyed fellowship with this fine group of believers just like Paul mentioned--For ***your fellowship in the gospel from the first day until now.*** (Philippians 1:5)

WE FOUND IT

---◆---

Pastor Dave Piper greeted us when we arrived at Grace Baptist Church in Kennewick, Washington. Pastor Piper had invited us to his church as missionaries to Brazil, and now that we represented Shepherds, he scheduled us to give a report to his church.

Pastor Dave showed us where to park in a wonderful place next to the educational wing of the church. There was a good hook-up for electricity and water and even a dump station there. What a handy place to park our fifth wheel trailer! The pastor gave me a key so we could use the facilities inside the church if we desired.

What happened next was not what we expected. In all the excitement of hooking up the trailer and settling in for the night, the church key was missing. I had lost it. This was so unlike me, as I am usually very careful with things. I honestly did not know what happened. That night I did a lot of praying but was unable to get much sleep. Margie and I have many stories about answered prayer.

The next morning, I was ashamed to mention to the pastor that I had lost the key. As I prayed about it more, I knew I had to give this problem completely to the Lord. I looked all over inside the trailer, but to no avail. How do you find a small metal key? I stepped outside, and to my utter delight, gazed down, and there it was. Thank you, Lord. That made the rest of our stay at the church more pleasant. James gave some good words about not having answers to prayer; our prayer-lessness rebuked us. Oh, yes, we prayed, but I wonder how earnest we were. ***You lust and do not have. You murder and covet and cannot obtain. You fight and war. Yet you do not have because you do not ask.*** (James 4:2)

A TRICK TO EVERY TRADE

TRAILER AWNING TROUBLE

Owning a fifth wheel trailer is not without its *hitch-es*--no pun intended. (Really?) The warmer weather of Southern California or Arizona was challenging. Not only did we use our evaporative coolers, but the trailer awning was a great asset. Initially I watched a gentleman activate the awning on his rig. The macho response is "Yes, I see how you do it, and I understand". The trouble was, I did understand UNTIL I had to use ours.

It was a very hot day. A slight breeze was blowing, but it was hot. The sun was shining brightly on the fifth-wheel kitchen windows. I went out and went through the routine of getting the awning set up. It truly was a challenge. I thought I had paid close attention to the man who showed me how, but the truth was, I did not have a clue how to do it the right way.

Finally, I got the awning so it was protecting the trailer from the blazing sun. I was to learn, in subsequent openings of the awning, that there was much I did not know. No one had told me that heavy winds were very hard on the awning. So, little by little, I learned to cope with this awning and its supporting framework. Now with special screw stakes that I put in the lawn I could fasten the awning so it would be more secure in high winds. But now the constant flapping of the canvas on each side would almost drive us crazy. We learned, as owners of a fifth wheel, that the supply stores are full of gadgets that enable customers to make life more comfortable while living in a fifth wheel. An almost insignificant item (several of them) stopped the flapping for good. But these items add up cost-wise, so you must be sure you really need something, before you buy it.

We thought we had solved the awning problem, but we found out we had not. While retracting the awning, there were some steps that needed to be taken, but unfortunately, I did not learn them. First, I spent hours trying to get the awning folded against the trailer wall. I thought I was handy with things, but this was a humbling experience until I learned the ropes. (Again, no pun intended – oh yeah?) The day finally came when I could open and close the awning with not too much trouble. By the time I learned how to do it right, we sold the trailer. I agree with Paul, even though I am sure he was talking about something else. ***Not that I speak in regard to need, for I have learned in whatever state I am, to be content:*** *(*Philippians 4:11) We no longer need a trailer, but the eleven years we lived in one was a rich experience.

WE ONLY MET HER ONCE

In the city of Citrus Heights, California, we presented the Shepherds ministry at Pioneer Baptist Church. Pastor Duty and his wife treated us to a delicious meal at a local restaurant that day. The folks in this church knew about Shepherds, but it had been many years since anyone had given an update on the ministry.

Something happened that day at Pioneer Baptist that would forever affect our lives for good. In our normal fellowship at this church, we were pleased to meet the believers who attended and showed an interest in our work. One of these people was Doris Jacobson. Little did we know how far that handshake and friendly visit with Doris would take us! She signed the clipboard that we always passed around, to receive the new Shepherds calendar that they mail out around Christmas time. Our email address was also available in case any wished to correspond with us.

It was not long until we received an email from Doris, saying how much she enjoyed our presentation and promising her interest in praying for us. We have exchanged many emails through the years. We learned from her that her son, Dr. Mark Jacobson, was a professor at Northwest Baptist Seminary. It is a small world, because we know him. Now we know his mother, Doris Jacobson. Besides this, Mark's wife

Catherine is the daughter of our well-known friend, Pastor George Cox.

When Doris wrote an email, it was a treasure. She has a unique way of expressing herself. We have kept all her letters, because they express the sweet, loving heart of a dear saint. Oh, how she loves Jesus and the work of the Lord! Every birthday or anniversary in our family, we received a special e-mail from her. She always talked about the Lord in her letters, and quoted many Scripture verses. When we sent special requests, she always responded with gratitude that we had asked her to pray about a special request.

In addition, Doris did something I doubt anyone else did. She printed our special prayer requests and hung them in conspicuous places in her home. This way she remembered to pray. What a jewel! Her unusual expressions were so refreshing that we loved to read and re-read her letters. We sent her a copy of our book *From a Canoe to a Chevy*, which she said she truly treasures. We are impressed with a fabulous woman who has already passed her ninety-fifth year (at the time this was written). We agree with Paul when he said of the Philippians*: I thank my God upon every remembrance of you,* (Philippians 1:3) Yes; we thank God for Doris Jacobson, who has been a special blessing in our lives. (Since writing this, her family informed us that Doris is in a care facility and no longer does email. For us an era has passed. We will write hard copy letters through the Post Office from now on.)

WHAT AN ATTRACTION!

We never cease to be amazed at God's handiwork in creation. For years, I have prefaced Bible study times with some interesting facts from the world of nature. The one I am telling now is both spectacular and annoying.

The Montana Regular Baptist Churches were gracious to Shepherds and allowed us to park our rig at their campsite at Lake Blaine. This is a beautiful lake close to Kalispell, Montana. In the summer, you expect all kinds of insects, and so as usual we met them. Each geographical location seems to have its own set of interesting creatures. We first recognized these particular creatures when they affixed themselves to the fifth wheel trailer screen door. It seems that when the weather was a little cooler, we saw them more often. Then we disgustingly found that when we were outside, these bugs enjoyed flying right at us, making us their landing strip. It was odd, and their peculiar behavior perplexed us.

Besides their obnoxious habit of attacking while flying, these bugs had a very unpleasant odor. In other words, we called them "stink bugs." They were not stinkbugs, but they did give off a disagreeable odor when disturbed. We tried to avoid them if possible so we did not trigger their stink mechanism. Later research revealed that these insects have complex systems. When the weather turns cooler, the bugs looked for warmer areas where they can live. They like to hibernate during the winter and emerge again in the spring. That is why I found them in our trailer many times, inadvertently disturbed them, and got the stinkbug treatment. Now I know why, when I was outside, these pests would attack me in the cool of the evening: they were looking for a warm place to land.

It is more complex than that. They have eight infrared sensors on their abdomen, which helps them find warm spots. That is why I never cease to be amazed at God's handiwork in nature. To think He created this little bug for a reason, and we marvel at His unique engineering. We will only know in heaven why God created all the amazing things He did. Take comfort in this verse: ***You are worthy, O Lord, to receive glory and honor and power; For You created all things, And by Your will they exist and were created.*** (Revelation 4:11)

WHAT AN ENTERPRISE

One of the many fascinating aspects of Shepherds Ministries is Shepherds Enterprises. This vital part of the ministry in Union Grove, Wisconsin, is to provide employment for adults with developmental disabilities by offering retailers an opportunity to carry the Shepherds products.

ENTERPRISE BUILDING - SHEPHERDS

When you enter this 15,000-feet production and warehouse facility, the size of it is overwhelming. The clients at this home are so good at what they do. They are diligent, energetic, motivated, and above all, cheerful in their work.

Local and other companies contract with Shepherds to do assembly work and a host of other necessary tasks to market their products. We saw a group of clients standing at a circular packaging machine. Each one placed part of the product in the bin in front of them. As the machine turned, a new part of the packaging was added, until the entire contents were heat-sealed and wrapped.

A wide variety of services takes place in this building, including the making of aromatic candles. The dexterity needed for placement of the wicks is noteworthy, and these clients do their work with pride and great efficiency.

Upon further questioning, we learned that we were not witnessing a slave labor camp situation. These workers received appropriate compensation for their tasks, and all work was according to the standards of any company who has employees. We were proud of being part of an organization with such lofty standards.

We hope you can visit the campus and see this fine operation personally. You will be impressed. When we watched these dear folks work, Paul's verse came to mind. (1Corinthians 10:31) ***Therefore, whether you eat or drink, or whatever you do, do all to the glory of God.***

A SOLO MESSAGE

When I was pastor of First Baptist Church in Ferndale, Washington, a family attended our church by the name of Bowman. Archie and Sylvia were faithful members, and she was a soloist. We loved her southern accent, and especially the way she sang hymns. Many times at musical communions, regular church services, and funerals, I requested her to sing.

The years flew by, and now they lived in Spokane. They were our host family when we were in the Spokane area. We appreciated so much their fellowship. Archie invited us to park alongside his garage and provided electricity and water for our fifth wheel trailer. They were very generous in their help to us while we were on the road.

At the Opportunity Baptist Church in Spokane, the pastor invited me to present the Shepherds ministry. We had been in this church several times. They were supportive of Shepherds and gladly invited us when we were in the area. On this Sunday evening, I showed the Power Point, preached, and showed a video of the Shepherds ministry.

As the leader closed the service, he requested a beautiful hymn. He then made an appeal for Shepherds in both prayer and finances. I had an instant thought as we were singing. Sitting in the rear of the church were Archie and Sylvia Bowman. They had come to hear about our Shepherds ministry. Immediately I thought of Sylvia's voice. I raised my hand, and the leader allowed me to introduce Sylvia to the congregation. I mentioned that she had sung many times in the church in Ferndale when I was pastor. Sylvia, disabled and not able to stand, sat and sang a verse of the designated song. Her beautiful voice filled the auditorium without a microphone. Every time she sang, she preached a message; every word and thought was very meaningful. The church appreciated greatly her participation that night. Thank God for people like her who use their talents for Christ. *As each one has received a gift, minister it to one another, as good stewards of the manifold grace of God.* (1 Peter 4:10)

A TRIP DOWN MEMORY LANE

W hat a thrill it was to travel into Tucson, Arizona, for some Shepherd meetings. We were visiting churches I had never heard of. As a youth, I had attended a larger church when our youth group went to this town. Now we were in unknown territory, and Pastor Smith invited us to his church, Sahuaro Baptist, to present Shepherds.

A plus for this visit was the full hookup for our trailer. This was always a concern, and when they were available, it was wonderful. In fact, they invited us to park there and stay as long as we desired.

One of the services we attended at this church, a man named Sidney Darling sang a beautiful solo, *"He Touched Me."* I pondered his name for a while and then remembered that years ago, when I was a young person, I traveled from Phoenix to our campsite in Prescott, Arizona. Our fellowship of churches was building the camp, and I could help a little in the project. As a young person, I was happy to be involved in this project.

However, the name ***Darling*** kept ringing a bell in my mind. I remembered a fair-sized man by that name with a huge mustache who drove a tan colored Chevrolet utility van. He was a plumber and drove from Tucson to do much of the water system at camp.

I asked Sidney Darling if anyone in his family fit that description. To my amazement, he immediately said, "That was my dad", and yes, he had a tan Chevrolet utility van.

Wow! Sixty-two years later, we meet his son, whom we had not known. What a small world! Exciting encounters like this happen from time to time, and we thank the Lord for the memories He gives us. In addition, I had the privilege of following up on some precious memories of years passed by. I remember the verse which states: (Isaiah 46:9) ***Remember the former things of old, For I am God, and there is no other; I am God, and there is none like Me.*** It was indeed good to remember people and God's goodness as we walked life's journey.

WHEN THE TOWING SERVICE DID NOT WORK

M any stories can be told of times we called the towing service to help us out of various situations. We were very happy to have two companies to which we belonged. Before we started with Shepherds, we were members of AAA services. It was a great security to have them available when needed. We used them many times. The other towing company we appreciated was Good Sam. This company had special services for those with RV's and motor homes. It was a comfort to know they were within calling distance most of the time.

We encountered an unusual situation at our home as we were preparing the trailer for departure. We were all packed and the truck hooked to the trailer when it started to snow. It snowed a lot, and it was obvious we were stuck in our spot alongside our house. I tried all "the tricks of the trade," but we were unable to move. I used carpet under the tires, and all sorts of wooden wedges, but nothing worked. All we got were spinning truck tires on snow and ice.

I called AAA, and within an hour, they were here to look at the situation. It was then we learned something about our service that surprised us. The AAA tow truck driver told us we should read the fine print on our contract. Well, who has a copy of that hanging around? I asked him to explain it to me. He said that AAA only gives aid to vehicles stranded and stuck in localities away from their homes. I asked him to wait while I went inside the house. I quickly called the other road service, Good Sam, who told me the same thing.

Now what should we do? We belong to two reliable towing services, but neither can move us from our snow-bound spot alongside our house. We had a predicament. In desperation, but not frantic, I called our Allstate insurance salesperson, a friend of mine. He figured out a brilliant plan that worked. He instructed me to request towing services from the AAA because they were already there and hooked up. Then he told me to tell the AAA man that Allstate would reimburse them for getting us out of our yard.

Have you ever heard of anything more complicated? However, it all worked out well. Allstate, our insurance, paid an AAA tow truck to get us out of our driveway. The AAA truck could have done it, but our policy prohibited it. Therefore, Allstate came to our rescue, and how thankful we were. We learned a great lesson that day. Even when we thought we were secure, we were not. Because we were home, it cancelled our privilege of getting service. We really appreciated the slogan, "You are in good hands with Allstate". A Scripture verse about hands has been a comfort to us: ***My times are in Your hand; Deliver me from the hand of my enemies, and from those who persecute me.*** Psalm 31:15

AN EXIT STRATEGY

EXIT GLACIER–ALASKA

Normally this has to do with warfare or a drill for the Fire Department. However, when we were in Alaska representing Shepherds, we scheduled a meeting in the town of Seward. At the church, we were pleased to give an update of our Shepherds ministry.

Because it was difficult to view a glacier, Margie and I thought it would be impossible for us to get close to one while in Alaska. Someone asked if we were going to visit Exit Glacier in that area while in Seward. We knew nothing about it, so we started doing research. To our delight, we discovered it was possible to make a side trip and get pretty close to this mass of ice and snow.

As I recall, it was approximately eight miles to the starting point at the Exit Glacier Nature Center. From this building, several trails lead to different places to view the glacier. We chose one that would bring us as close as possible to the mass of ice we wanted to see. The path was a challenge for two old people. Margie and I went arm in arm so I could help support her in this wet, sometimes slippery, cold walk to the glacier's edge. We talked with fellow hikers along the way who seemed to be amazed that at our age we were engaged in such a trek. It was fun, even though tiring. We were glad we had our raincoats, as it was raining that day. My two bionic knees have always cooperated well, for which I was thankful. It took a long time to make it to the lookout station. It was rewarding to reach this level of spectacular viewing. Margie rested while I went ahead to look into the massive ice caves. They are immense and are inching their way down the slope. When rested, she joined me for the remainder of this beautiful sight.

One trail led to the Glacier's Toe, the other to the Glacier's Edge. Both were spectacular and worth the time and effort to make it to that point. They told us not to get close, which meant going beyond the safety rails. The massive hunks of ice can break loose and crush a person in an instant. We appreciated this information.

Some folks told us this Exit Glacier begins up on the Harding ice fields. There, as much as 100 feet of snow can fall during the year. The immense pressure of this snow compresses after a few years and forms glacier ice. Truly, we were witnessing another miracle of God's great handiwork in nature. Job may not have been referring to glaciers, but his words come close to what we saw as we viewed these huge ice masses: ***The waters harden like stone, and the surface of the deep is frozen.*** (Job 38:30)

WHEN YOU LEAVE, PLEASE LOCK THE DOOR

S eldom did we ever encounter a situation like this. Cambria is a quaint, small town on Highway 1 in northern California between San Francisco and Los Angeles. We parked at First Baptist Church of Cambria, whose pastor was David Hollingsworth. Our meetings there were a blessing to us, and the folks said the same about us. We were invited to people's homes for very enjoyable meals. While in this general area, we visited the famous elephant seals along the beach, and one day scheduled a trip to Hearst Castle. That was an experience we will never forget.

The Baptist church is located along the highway and landscaped with beautiful bushes and flowers. The church's stained-glass windows are a sight to behold. They are attractive both on the inside and out. We really enjoyed our time there.

The place we parked the trailer was a challenge to back into, as it was alongside the building. As I remember, we had a full hookup, water and sewer, which was a luxury for us. While we were at the church, a couple invited us for a meal at The Hometown Café in Cambria. This couple were very interested in our Shepherds ministry, and we were very happy to tell them all we could about the home. We were intrigued with the scope of this couple's travels and the things they had done in past days.

CREEKSIDE RESTAURANT, CAMBRIA, CA

That night in the café, there were many customers enjoying their meals. Our conversation just kept on going like the "Energizer bunny." I looked around and noticed the customers were thinning out. We were not the hosts, so I kept quiet about our soon being alone in the building. But that is exactly what happened. Finally, the noise in the kitchen stopped, and a man quietly walked to our table. He spoke to our hosts, and then I realized what an unusual situation we were experiencing. The owner of the café addressed our hosts by name and kindly asked them to take our time visiting, but as you leave please lock the door. "Thanks for patronizing us, and have a good evening." We continued our very long evening, and when it was over we put our dishes in the kitchen, walked out, and our friend locked the door. I imagine none of you has had an experience like that. I'm not really sure our host even paid the bill, but he probably did that the next day. Job's word comes to mind when I think of this delightful experience in Cambria. ***Let me be weighed on honest scales, That God may know my integrity.*** (Job 31:6)

WHERE DO I PUT THE DISPLAY?

DISPLAY BY PULPIT

In every church we visited for Shepherds, we put up a display that included appropriate literature and pictures of the home and some of the clients. When arranging for our meetings, we always included a request for a table on which we could display our Shepherds material.

Occasionally the person in charge did have a table set up when we arrived, and that was much appreciated. Many times, I would go with the pastor through a maze of hallways, doorways, and rooms to a dark room filled with tables. Then we would make our way back to the foyer carrying this unbelievably heavy table. I am so glad my two bionic knees never ached after such table transfers.

In some churches, large tables were not available, so we would have the display board overlap over the edges of a table that was much too small to hold everything. However, praise the Lord, one way or another it was possible to display our literature. The position of these tables varied greatly. Some were in places that completely ignored the flow of people as they exited the building, so hardly anyone saw or took the literature. In one church, we had to put our display outside the church, because that was the only place available. I prayed the wind would not blow, making an airplane of every piece of paper on the table.

In one small church, the only place to put the table was in the far-left corner as one looked toward the pulpit. But you know, it worked well. After the service, people swarmed up there to see what there was. We discovered that in that church it would make no difference where the table was. The pastor was the one that set the pace, and it was refreshing. It was always thrilling to visit the churches and tell people what God was doing at Shepherds. The Apostle Paul said it best to express our feelings as we went to each church: ***But I know that when I come to you, I shall come in the fullness of the blessing of the gospel of Christ.*** (Romans 15:29)

WHERE'S THE LAUNDROMAT?

———————◆———————

Every Friday while on the road, we tried to get our clothes washed. We would normally relocate to a new place each Thursday. After setting up, we looked for a laundromat. We did this on the Internet usually. I would get our system working and then use the laptop to search for an adequate place. After finding several places, I recorded the addresses and then went to inspect them. I tried to find the clean ones, and when I found a good one, Margie went to look it over.

Can you imagine how many places we used in those years? Some were very nice, but others were deplorable. Some had hot water, but others did not. In a very affluent town in California, we kept feeding quarters into the slot and were perplexed why it was costing so much. We figured it had something to do with that town. As we were feeding the machine, a couple entered the place, and I thought they could be the owners. I asked them if there was something wrong with the machine, because I had to put so much money into it before it would operate. The answer I got was most unusual. She told me that we had the water control on HOT water. "Here, you pay depending on the water temperature."" We were amazed; that was a first for us.

We learned that laundromats are a variety of social clubs. You meet all kinds of people, and we witnessed to folks there. One time we met a man who was fleeing from his home and wife. He was in desperate spiritual need. I had prayer with him. We convinced him to change his mind, return to his family, and start all over again. He agreed, and we were happy.

When we were in a town for several days, we would go to the laundromat early to get our favorite machines. Each week when we did our grocery shopping, I went to the courtesy counter and purchased quarters for our next trip to the laundromat. We made some interesting friends during our years of frequenting laundromats in various places.

Some laundromats were very decrepit; others, because of vandalism, were in shambles. Some were in a dangerous part of town and unsafe to enter. Some coin machines were damaged by thieves and were not functional. We were careful to evaluate how safe it was to be in a place. The modern ones were a delight, because they used modern technology. One place in Fresno, California, took no coins, but used a modern computerized credit card.

Because we never knew how people handled the tables in each place, we took plastic to cover the tables on which we folded our clothes. At one place in Kingman, Arizona, I saw the person in charge folding a fitted sheet. I watched her closely and learned how she did it. I had gone online to find some help before this, but to see a person folding it was a tremendous help.

There is a verse from the story of Jesus' transfiguration with which every person who washes clothes can relate. ***His clothes became shining, exceedingly white, like snow, such as no launderer on earth can whiten them.*** (Mark 9:3) When sinners trust Jesus as their Savior, this is what He does for them. He makes them whiter than snow and forgives them.

STRONG WINDS

On this day, we traveled Interstate 10 across Arizona and California. Pulling a 30-foot trailer is not such a chore for any driver. It always takes plenty of gas to get from point A to B, however. Finding the right place to stop for gas and meals was always a challenge.

As we drove along that day, suddenly I noticed the window and some object fly right out of the rig ahead of us. What happened, I thought to myself. Then suddenly I realized a fierce wind had arisen and the pressure blew that trailer window out. The automatic transmission on our truck started to get sluggish. I pressed more on the gas pedal, but our speed was getting less. We had not experienced high winds thus far in our travels, but after this day, we could no longer say that. Being comparatively new at driving this way, there were lessons we had to learn as we went.

Gradually, then faster, our speed slowed way down. I put the transmission in lower gear, and with all the gas I dared give it, we were going about 25 miles per hour. Stopping along this stretch of the highway was out of the question. We continued on, praying as we went. The Lord helped us, and we gave Him the glory for allowing us to make it to our destination that day. Four tons of metal going just 25 miles an hour speaks volumes of God's might in the world of nature. When God sends a wind, men listen. The Apostle Paul on his trip to

Rome encountered much worse conditions than we ever had. ***When we had put to sea from there, we sailed under the shelter of Cyprus, because the winds were contrary,*** (Acts 27:4) When the winds in your life are contrary, commit your way to the Lord and allow Him to work it out.

YEARLY VISIT TO SHEPHERDS

ENTRANCE SIGN TO SHEPHERDS

A s representatives, we met yearly on campus for orientation, instruction and fellowship. For Margie and me
it was very special, because we could visit our daughter Joy.
These meetings allowed us to receive updates from the different departments at Shepherds, and this in turn helped
with our ministry among the churches.

Dr. William Amstutz, president of Shepherds, met with
staff in the morning for prayer time. This updated us on the
heartbeat of the physical, spiritual and financial needs of the
home. Dr. Amstutz also had another session where he gave
specific reports about the home and plans for future days.
These were always very inspirational, and Dr. Amstutz, in his

quiet, unassuming manner, blessed us with his words. We praise the Lord for his leadership at Shepherds and the spiritual emphasis he maintains.

Mr. Dan DiDonato, Vice Chairman for Development, met with us about financial matters, and he was very helpful in teaching us how to present this concern to churches. We greatly valued his advice and wisdom. Dan surprised me when he flew to Bellingham, Washington, right after my double knee surgery. He presented me with a beautiful fruit basket and an accompanying card from Shepherds.

Mr. Alan Pick, head of Church relations, met with all the representatives to give suggestions and help on how to get meetings. He also provided material to help with our ministry presentations. Mr. Pick was a personal blessing. He was an encourager, and he called us regularly to help us do our best in representing Shepherds. I was accountable mostly to Mr. Pick and Dan DiDonato, whom I considered my "bosses" in this great ministry.

The interpersonal fellowship during this yearly visit was very special for Margie and me. We learned how other representatives were doing their ministry, and they heard our story as well. We were on a different work agreement than the other representatives. We attended the meetings in December each year. To finalize the week, Shepherds had a Christmas banquet to thank all the employees at the home. A church volunteered help by coming on campus to be with the residents so all the counselors and workers could attend the banquet. The food was delicious and the program well planned. It was winter, so we had quite a lot of inclement weather through the years.

The sweet spirit that existed among all who were connected to Shepherds impressed us. It was a blessing to go there yearly for these meetings and then come back to represent Shepherds in the churches. King David expressed our feelings in this verse: ***Behold, how good and how pleasant it is for brethren to dwell together in unity!*** (Psalm 133:1)

YOU NEVER KNOW WHAT
THEY WILL SAY

———◆———

We never cease to be amazed at what happened as we represented Shepherds Ministries in many churches on the west coast. The wide variety of people we met was inspirational, to say the least.

We were in a church that was well attended but very far from any town. Sometimes we wondered how churches got started in places like this. However, when we saw the large attendance and great activity of the church, there was no doubt in our minds.

In the morning, we presented Shepherds in both Sunday School and the morning service. There was great interest in what we said about Shepherds. Margie always had a ministry with folks at the literature table. Many times, families, women, would share with Margie the burden of their heart about a family member who had intellectual difficulties. Margie always felt this was one of her ministries as we traveled.

After the morning service, a man approached me who was obviously a genius with numbers. He questioned some facts that he saw on the Shepherds video. I accepted his comments, but it did not disturb me, because I knew the president of Shepherds was not giving out incorrect data in the video.

In some ways, the gentleman who spoke to me really wanted to say something else. After his long discourse about the matter on the video, he then said: "Your president, Dr. William Amstutz, has good taste. He is wearing my identical tie. Sure enough, they did match. He was feeling good that he and Dr. Amstutz had the same tastes. I concluded that anything negative that may have been in his mind was erased by the episode of "the matching ties." Jesus said it best in these words: ***"For by your words you will be justified, and by your words you will be condemned."*** (Matthew 12:37)

YUKKY IN YUCCA VALLEY

CALVARY BAPTIST, YUCCA VALLEY, CA

The title of this story has nothing to do with this lovely town. It is what happened while we were there that provokes the title of this chapter. Going to a church we had never visited was an enjoyable experience. This was the case at the Baptist Church in Yucca Valley, CA. It was quite a trip to get there, but we found it with no problem. As was our custom, we went to the church office, introduced ourselves, and asked where we could park our rig. It was very important for us to set up before dark.

We backed into our spot and finally hooked into the electrical system. We were glad that initial part was finished before it got dark. What happened after this was amazing.

During the night, it started to rain, and the wind was fierce. Our fifth wheel trailer was swaying in the strong wind. The rain pounded against the aluminum siding, sounding almost like a gunshots. This storm reminded us of traveling in a big airplane when we encountered a storm. The thrashing around and tremendous tumult was almost overwhelming.

In the morning, it was still raining, and even though we were in the desert, it was cold. What I saw amazed me. Looking out at the church parking lot, there appeared to be a huge pile of sand. I had never experienced anything quite like this. The heavy rains had washed tons of sand from the canyons and ravines onto the parking lot. The church got help from the city in backhoeing tons of sand into trucks. This process was very complicated.

The rains continued, and because the main rush of water came along one side of the church's parking lot, it was dangerously close to the entrance and all the church windows. Because of the huge sand deposits, the level had risen to two feet and made new paths for the rushing water. This brought raging water to the windowsills, and with the continued force, water had made its way through the sealed windows. The inside of the church filled with water. Rugs were soaked and ruined, and the rising water was damaging the wooden pews.

We were experiencing a disaster before our eyes. Water was gushing down in torrents from higher elevations, and it seems the church parking lot was the meeting place for it all. Volunteers worked tirelessly through the night and all the next day. To make matters worse, the next night there was another flood and it all happened again. It was sad to see the parking lot fill up again with tons of sand. Barricades helped keep another rush of water from entering the church; however, water channels cut through the tons of sand, and it still made things a mess.

The church took this disaster in stride and coped well with all the damage. The next meeting in this building was somber, but they rejoiced in the way the Lord had enabled them to accept the excesses of sand and water. We had a wonderful time there, and they received the message of Shepherds with gratitude. They were supporters of this ministry, and it was a delight to bring them an update. We often think of the Lord's statement about rain as His blessing when we need it: ***That you may be sons of your Father in heaven; for He makes His sun rise on the evil and on the good, and sends rain on the just and on the unjust***. (Matthew 5:45) And we know that in some cases we may get more than we think we really need, but we must trust the Lord's sovereignty.

SURPRISED BY A BIG ONE

During our Shepherds ministry in Anchorage, I kept looking for wildlife so I could take pictures. Murphy's Law was working overtime. I looked, and there were no animals nearby so I could photograph them.

The local people told many stories about large animals, and it was interesting to hear homeowners lament that these big animals came into their yards and destroyed things. That is the way it is in Alaska. One day while we were visiting with friends, the host opened the garage door, and there walking on his driveway was a large moose. I raced for my camera and succeeded in capturing the event, which made me very happy. I thought this was the only shot I would get of a moose.

MOOSE IN FRONT YARD

While in Anchorage, we read and heard stories of several incidents with moose and cars having an encounter. Thankfully, we still were not able to see one up close. We were aware that it would not be wise to try to get near one of these big ones, especially if it was a female with a baby moose. We waited, but knew it was not going to happen. THEN it did!

One morning I went out to warm the car up before Margie joined me on a quick trip to the grocery store. I was alone in the car, at the driver's seat, and the engine was running normally. Without any warning, I sensed something out of the corner of my eye. As I looked to my left, slightly to the rear of the car, there was my longed-for chance. A mother moose with her baby came from the street and entered the churchyard, heading for the back of the church where there was underbrush and trees. Fortunately, I carried my Nikon camera with me all the time. I readied it for a shot or two and rolled down the window as the animals slowly walked by the car. They were very close. It was a great opportunity for a good shot; I was thrilled! A professional photographer would have desired a more posed shot, but I was eminently satisfied with what I saw. The pictures came out looking good, so I was pleased; I was finally able to get my picture! For those who live in Anchorage, our eagerness to see one of these critters was probably not understood. However, we thoroughly enjoyed that opportunity to take our own picture of God's miracle in nature. Later, on a visit, I caught moose coming right into the yard. I show that one above.

We never cease to be amazed at God's handiwork in nature. He created all, and we enjoyed much of that creation as we read and traveled. ***I know all the birds of the mountains, and the wild beasts of the field are Mine***. (Psalm 50:11)

AN AMAZING ENCOUNTER

A n amazing thing happened when we were parked at the First Baptist Church of Polson, Montana. Mr. Al Pick, the man under whom I worked at Shepherds, was director of Church Relations. His daughter met a young man, and they decided to get married in Cut Bank, Montana.

We were already traveling to different points in Montana while parked at this church in our fifth wheel trailer. Even though Cut Bank is quite a trip from Polson, Margie and I decided to attend the wedding. We started very early in the morning, because we would have to cross Marias Pass at the Continental Divide at 5,280 feet in Glacier National Park. The scenery is breathtaking for those who love mountain vistas. I always took plenty of pictures on our trips, even though we did not stop. That would delay us too much, so I just took the shots through the truck windows.

The weather was hot, but thankfully, there were no strong winds or storms. I say that because the locals told us the wind was so strong during some storms in Cut Bank that it blew trains off the tracks. That is a lot of wind, but we are thankful we did not experience this. We arrived at the wedding place in time to use the restrooms, where we dressed for the wedding. What a joy it was to see the Pick family, their children, and several others. The service was very nice, and we were able to stay for some of the reception before returning home.

It was midafternoon, and we had about 180 miles to go over the mountains and across the plains. In a way, it was hard to say goodbye to our friends, because we were not sure when we would see them again. We had many special memories as we drove home and were thankful there were no storms or delays. We were so happy we had made the decision to attend this wedding. Because of time and job changes we have not seen the newlyweds since. They live in another part of Montana and are very happy in their church and work. Our trip to Cut Bank that day reminded us of Paul's words to the Romans. ***That I may come to you with joy by the will of God, and may be refreshed together with you.*** (Romans 15:32) It was indeed refreshing for us to be with these dear friends for their wedding. We hope you enjoy the company of others and thank God when He makes it possible.

A PRACTICAL GIFT FROM OUR SON

⸺◆⸺

Our son always amazed us in his choice of gifts to us. The year he gave us a Nikon camera was memorable. We used it most of the years we worked for Shepherds, and we still take pictures with it. It is battle-worn and scarred but in good working condition. Another practical gift was a GPS (Global Positioning System).

Because I am not as up-to-date as the younger generation, there were aspects of this new unit which I did not know how to use. At first, I could not figure out how to get my address into the machine so it would direct us to our destination. One day in Tucson, Arizona, I gave up and went into one of the branch stores where he had purchased it, and asked some questions. I specifically asked the clerk how to put in the starting direction. I will never forget his astute answer. He advised me that the home address was not necessary. He assured me that this unit knows your home address; all it wants to know is where you are going. From then on, I never had any more trouble.

On the road, this system was such a blessing and help in our work. I remember going along Highway 101 on the California coast. We were hungry and wanted to find a place to stop. Not being acquainted with the area where we were traveling, I *asked* the GPS, which we lovingly gave the name "Susie," where the restaurants were in the city we were approaching. Susie gave a list of places, we chose one, and it directed us right to the door. It helped us turn off the freeway and make right and left turns until we were directly in front of the restaurant of our choice. What a machine! In the Los Angeles area, we had a meeting in a church in Long Beach. We parked our fifth wheel in San Dimas at the time. With the old system of paper maps, it would have been a colossal task to find our way to the church. Margie was always my co-pilot, and now with Susie, we traveled on five different freeways. It was a miracle how this little machine which fits in the palm of our hand, helped us find our way.

We thanked the Lord many times for this service. We laughed, because we learned to know how Susie would direct us and when she would tell us to make a right turn, and how many feet it would be before stopping at the next intersection. It was a lot of fun, and we will always thank Rawlie, our son, for such a practical gift. This was our prayer each time we used the machine: ***Now may our God and Father Himself, and our Lord Jesus Christ, direct our way to you.*** (1Thessalonians 3:11)

AN EMOTIONAL DEDICATION

---◆---

God always has fresh, interesting, and amazing things as we serve Him. Close to Ferndale, in the town of Nooksack, a church invited us for a Shepherds presentation. As usual, we arrived early to set up the display table. We also checked with audio-visual concerning the Power Point and video parts of the service. All went as planned.

We have been friends of this church for many years. We first knew it because the pastor was our friend. Later, as missionaries, we gave reports when home from Brazil. After our years on the field, First Baptist Church of Ferndale, Washington, called me as pastor, and we continued this relationship. When we began our ministry for Shepherds, our contact with this church continued.

It was nice to be in a church where we knew many people. This morning they were very receptive to the message of Shepherds. We were grateful for their kindness shown in not only prayer support but also financial support to this wonderful Christian home for the mentally disabled. At the conclusion of this Sunday service, we expected the pastor would close with prayer. However, this did not happen. He made an impassioned plea for his people to support Margie and me in the ministry we were representing. When Pastor Hardinger first came to this church, I had the privilege of inviting him out for a sundae, officially welcoming him to our area. Even though we had not been able to have a lot of fellowship, I knew he appreciated this initial greeting.

At any rate, this morning's service conclusion was special. He wanted to show us how much he and the church appreciated our ministry with Shepherds. He called Margie and me up front to the pulpit. After giving some words of encouragement, he said he was going to have a word of prayer for us as we continued our travels and ministry for Shepherds. THEN he asked anyone in attendance to feel free to come forward and encircle us as he prayed. We stepped down from the platform, and people quietly started to surround us. Some placed their hands on us, others held our hands, and still others lightly touch our shoulders or head. As the pastor prayed, we could feel the Lord's power in the room. It was an emotional time, and one we will never forget as he poured out his heart to the Lord on our behalf. This pastor's spontaneous action constituted one of the most precious moments we had in our ministry.

Thank God for men who encourage their people as he did. ***The effective, fervent prayer of a righteous man avails much.*** (James 5:16)

AN INVITATION BEYOND EXPECTATIONS

M r. Dan DiDonato, Vice President of Shepherds Foundation, had visited Anchorage and neighboring cities earlier and had been impressed by the great reception he received to the Shepherd's ministry. He visited some donors to the ministry and thought it would be good for Margie and me to have meetings in some of the churches.

Representatives have to start very early in the year to schedule meetings. It takes a long time, with repeated phone calls and emails, to secure meetings. I started in Anchorage, a central place, and then contacted churches in surrounding towns.

We set up dates that would be compatible with driving and living conditions in that region. I phoned Dimond Boulevard Baptist Church, and Pastor Andy Frey answered the phone. He was friendly, warm, and very open to having us come and share the ministry with their church family. We selected a date when we could be at his church, and I thanked him cordially for the gracious invitation.

DIMOND BAPTIST - ANCHORAGE

Then he asked me where we would be staying while in Anchorage. At that early point in our scheduling, I did not have a clue where we would be living. Pastor Andy quickly warned me that our time in Anchorage corresponded with the hunting season. He then informed me that if we were thinking of staying in a motel or hotel, the nightly price would be extremely high. We had not even thought of this. It would be hundreds of dollars per night. My heart sank as he told me this. We really did not know what to do. As I was pondering aloud with pastor Frey on the phone, he interjected this: "Dimond Boulevard Baptist Church is going to give you a place to stay while here. You will live in one of the rooms of the church we have provided." I was completely overwhelmed with his kind offer. He had never seen us, nor knew anything about us, but was offering housing while in his city. In the midst of my thanks to him for this gracious offer, he added another that was beyond our fondest imaginations. He assured me that while in Anchorage, their church would also provide transportation. I could scarcely believe it. Imagine, in one phone call, we had received an invitation to speak in their church and be given free housing and transportation. We praise the Lord for such special people God programmed into our lives. This church in Anchorage certainly exemplified the true meaning of this verse: *Do not forget to entertain strangers, for by so doing some have unwittingly entertained angels*. (Hebrews 13:2)

AN OPPORTUNITY MISSED FOREVER

···◆···

M y missionary brother Ernie's *angels,* as he called them, had secretly arranged a surprise 80th birthday celebration for him. They also funded my airfare to Singapore so I could attend this memorable event. All was set on this side of the ocean, and Siang, Ernie and Verda's goddaughter, took care of things over there.

On the morning of departure, I was at my computer printing the boarding passes. I was going to drive to our son's home, and he would take us to the airport. All went well until I made an unbelievable discovery while printing the boarding pass. I discovered that the airplane which we should have been on was leaving the SeaTac airport in Seattle headed for Singapore at that very moment. For some unknown reason, I had not read the plane schedule correctly. The plane was to leave Seattle at 12:55 PM. For reasons I will never understand, I inadvertently related the departure time to nighttime instead of mid-day. What a fool I made of myself! I have never had such an empty feeling pass over me. I had goofed, and there was no correction for my mistake. It was completely my fault, and I understood that.

I drove to our son's house, and we went to the airport to see what I could do. One of the attendants was not very kind about my mistake with the airlines. I did not blame her. I had made a terrible mistake. We went over all options, and there was no way we would ever make it to Singapore in time for my brother's birthday celebration. By this time, I had learned that the event was not a total surprise to my brother, so I phoned and asked him if I should cancel our trip. He wanted us to come to Singapore, so arrangements were made, and you can be sure I read the plane ticket correctly and was on time for the flight.

The sixteen-hour flight to Singapore went well. All I can say is that it is a long time to be in one airplane. What a joy to be in my brother's home again! I lamented the fact that we had missed his birthday party but was thankful we could help him celebrate several days later. As usual, they entertained us, instead of my doing it for them. We had a wonderful time, and I thanked my brother's dear friends who made our trip possible.

RIDE ON A SINGAPORE TRISHAW

Singapore is a delightful place, so full of history and sites, very enjoyable to any visitor. Margie and I had previously been to some of these places. The number of places they took us for meals was amazing, and we thoroughly enjoyed them. It was also nice to attend my brother's Bible classes while in Singapore and to worship at Grace Baptist, a church started with his help many years ago. Time does not seem to help me forget the goof I made that day long ago, and in some ways, it seems I will never live it down. Missing an important birthday is not a good thing, but there is something more important that no one should ever miss. That is the day of salvation. Paul warns us with this word: ***For He says, In an acceptable time, I have heard you, And in the day of salvation, I have helped you. Behold, now is the accepted time; behold, now is the day of salvation.*** (2 Corinthians 6:2)

AN UNEXPECTED FRIENDSHIP

Ralph and Margie Poulson were representing Shepherds in a new state. In Montana, we parked our rig at Lake Blaine Bible Camp. We were very grateful for a place to park our fifth wheel trailer.

Across from where we parked at camp was the large dining hall. At one end, there were two upstairs apartments, used by missionaries and speakers. We noticed a pick-up truck with a camper parked at the side entrance to the hall. A man was sleeping in the camper, and later we learned that his wife was sleeping in the missionary apartment. During the day, we occasionally saw them come and go from the dining room. Finally, it was our delight to meet them and be better acquainted. They told us they were using the camp facility prior to moving into their renovated home.

Over the ensuing weeks, we became friends. Ken & Doris Hall were old-timers around those parts, and Ken had held important jobs during their years in Montana. We were intrigued with the fascinating stories he told about his work with big machinery and many other activities. He and Doris were faithful Christians, attending Bethel Baptist Church in Kalispell, Montana.

A special bonding took place between the Halls and us. As time marched on, we stayed in contact via e-mail and telephone conversations. When we returned to Montana for more Shepherds meetings, we wanted to be sure to see Ken and Doris as often as possible. One day we were shocked when Doris called to say Ken had died. We knew them only a short time, but it seemed we had been friends forever.

Our hearts went out to dear Doris, who was now alone and suffering from severe allergies. Fortunately, her children and Christian friends gave her the support she needed. Margie has stayed in contact with her all through the years since we first met. It was always a joy to meet her when we were in Montana for meetings. Doris, in advanced years, is really a friend and inspiration to us. She never complained, although she certainly had opportunity to do so. She is witty, computer perceptive, and very vibrant in her conversation on the phone or in person. We love her. This verse is widely interpreted in many ways, but we use it because Ken and Doris Hall were faithful friends, and what a joy it was to be with them. ***A man who has friends must himself be friendly, But there is a friend who sticks closer than a brother.*** (Proverbs 18:24)

AN UNUSUAL CONTACT
FOR SHEPHERDS

S cheduling meetings is the ongoing work for the Shepherds representatives. We received many wonderful hints from Mr. Alan Pick, Director of Church Relations for Shepherds. At our yearly meetings, other representatives suggested ways they made contacts with churches. We took them all seriously, knowing this would be our ministry and we needed to know as much as possible. Thankfully, we had been missionaries to Brazil and as a result could contact the churches we had visited during those years. It was a wonderful advantage for us.

We discovered it was best to try to schedule our meetings at least eight to ten months ahead of our calendar year. This required using every tool at our disposal. We did, and spent multiplied hours on the phone and at the laptop securing meetings. It was amazing how long it took to receive an answer from a church secretary or pastor to request a meeting. However, normally the meetings came in, and when we started each January, our calendar was pretty well filled with commitments for the year, minus the major holidays.

While we were in the process of seeking meetings, my brother Ernie and his wife Verda and their goddaughter Siang contacted us asking if we had any meetings lined up in Great

Falls, Montana. Koh Siang Kiang, their Chinese goddaughter, had studied at Dallas Theological Seminary, receiving her Doctor of Christian Education degree. We were privileged to attend her graduation, which was a wonderful experience. I told her we had no contacts in that city. She replied that she had studied with a man who was the pastor of a church in Montana. She told me to contact him and tell him that she had recommended us for a Shepherds meeting. To make a longer story shorter, he did invite us to come to his church. What a wonderful time we had with him, his wife, and the church family! The church was very receptive to the Shepherds message, and we appreciated having this new contact. Before we visited his church, we talked on the phone several times. In the conversations, I remembered Paul's words to the Philippians: *But I trust in the Lord that I myself shall also come shortly.* **(Philippians 2:24)**

What a joy it was to share Shepherds with them and others, because it meant so much to us.

AN UPHILL CHALLENGE

When traveling with a truck and a trailer, you never know what experience may be around the next corner. A most challenging one came as we approached a city in California.

The normal route into the city and the church where we were going was under construction. I remembered a road that led to a friend's house nearby that perhaps would get us to our desired destination. I turned into the road leading to his house, and we made our way down the street to his driveway. Instead of going into his place, I continued ahead, hoping to come out at a road that would take us past the construction zone. As we got nearer, we got a shock by what we encountered.

This road had no outlet, but was a dead-end street. Previously we had seen no sign indicating this. We found ourselves in a precarious situation, and it was a very tense time for us. My only alternative was to go into our friend's driveway. The problem with this was the acute incline leading up to his house. However, we had now gone to the point of no return, and I must go up his driveway. The trailer is heavy, and I was secretly afraid the truck might not be able to pull the weight uphill at that steep incline. I prayed, asking the Lord to help me, and put the truck in its lowest gear and started the incline. It was almost too much for the truck engine, but turning back was impossible. With God's help, the great Ford engine got us to the top of the driveway where it leveled out and made a slight right turn. I knew that it led to an alley that would allow us to return to the main highway from which we had come. Turning to the right, we soon were shocked by a huge tree whose limbs prevented us from passing to the alley. Now what were we going to do? We were in a man's driveway and unable to go forward or backward.

By this time the owner of the house got up from his afternoon nap, awakened by the noise outside his house. Fortunately, he was a kind man, immediately saw our predicament, and grabbed a saw. He probably also wondered why I was in his driveway. On his ladder, he climbed up into the huge tree and started cutting limbs. These were not small twigs. I felt very foolish, having placed him in such a situation. He had to do a lot of cutting to make it possible for the trailer to pass this spot. Finally, the test came when without further problems the trailer was able to pass the tree and get into the alley. I gave him a good tip, grateful for his kindness in helping us out of a very difficult situation.

We had a wonderful time in the church where we spoke, and will not soon forget how we got there. I was so sure I knew a way to get there, but now you know I did not. This verse spoke volumes to me about my situation that day: ***Therefore let him who thinks he stands take heed lest he fall.*** (1 Corinthians 10:12) What a great lesson this was for us, and perhaps for you who read this story.

ANYTHING JUST TO SEE OUR CHILDREN!

W e were ministering in Montana when our son called and said he and his family were going to take a mini-vacation to Coeur d'Alene, Idaho. He wondered if we could meet them there for a few hours someday.

We thought and prayed about this and decided it would be fun. We left Polson, Montana, early for the long trip across miles of big-sky Montana and its beautiful scenery. After three hours of travel, we arrived at the motel where they were staying. It was nice to have the fellowship with our son Rawlie and his wife Gina; she had invited her mother and father, John and Doris Harder to come along.

It seemed almost like a dream that we were with our children for those precious hours. When mealtime came, they chose a nice steak house, and we all gathered for a meal to commemorate Margie's birthday. We had a super time together, and then they went back to their motel for a brief time. A glance at our watch reminded us we had better get back on the road and head for *home.* We said our goodbyes and headed east on Interstate 90 for Montana.

The trip home went well, and we spent the time recounting the joy we had with family. The route we selected took us through some mountains, along beautiful river roads, through lush meadows, great open fields, and miles and miles of driving in big-sky Montana. How we thanked the Lord for this safe trip of over 360 miles and six and a half hours of traveling in our Ford truck. It was very nice to get back to our fifth wheel trailer parked at the First Baptist Church in Polson. It was our home away from home. We finished the day reflecting on how good God was to us in giving us wonderful children and grandchildren. We agree with the Apostle John, who wrote, *I have no greater joy than to hear that my children walk in truth.* (3 John 1:4)

BACK UP

⸻ ◆ ⸻

After high school, I was a truck driver for the State of Arizona Educational Agency. I picked up war surplus material at many bases in California and brought them to the Fair Grounds in Phoenix, where the schools chose the things they wanted.

I must confess, I never learned well the art of backing a trailer. For some reason, it was always a chore. I had seasoned truckers help me with good suggestions, which aided me greatly. Arriving at a church, I was thrilled when the configuration was such that all I had to do was drive in frontwards to our parking place. However, that was not very often the case. I do not brag about it, but I am a determined person, so no matter how long it took me, I would get the trailer into the spot assigned for it. Margie would help as much as she could, guiding me with cell phone conversations. Even then, I am sure she was exhausted with my poor performance of getting into the slot.

I always figured Murphy's Law worked against me. Like the time we parked at our friends' home in Spokane and our host had a place next to his garage where I could tap into the electricity and water. The downside of this was that his driveway to our appointed spot was uphill. How many times did I try to make it through the gateway, just wide enough for our trailer, into the desired place? Complications always were present. This uphill driveway was a challenge every seven days when we made the trip to a trailer park to dump the waste tanks.

I remember vividly one night at a church in California. The church secretary showed us the spot where we could stay, and I started the lengthy process of trying to back into it. It was pitch black, and I could not see behind me. I hit a chain link fence and was sure I would have to pay the church for the damage. One of my favorite Scripture verses is ...***the Lord preserves the simple...*** (Psalm 116:6) Being simple, I know the Lord would help me. He always has. The fence was not terribly "hurt," and I was able to bring it back to shape so no one would ever know I hit it. Praise the Lord!

Unbelievably, our own home in Ferndale was the place it took the longest to get our trailer to its nest. I had to miss the edge of our garage with the jutting gutter trough and align the trailer with our house on top of the cement slab the men of our church had so graciously provided us. With the best of intentions, one afternoon while trying to get around that gutter, I slammed the edge of the trailer into it. I was desperate, got a sledgehammer, set the ladder in place, and gave that gutter a blow it will never forget. Problem solved (maybe).

As missionaries, we had plenty of back up with prayer and financial support. However, when Ralph wanted to back up the trailer, he was a flop. As the Lord spoke comfort to Moses, so he did to us so many times: ***"Now therefore, go, and I will be with your mouth and teach you what you shall say."*** (Exodus 4:12)

BIBLE ALPHABET

I n Brawley, California, we had meetings at the Western Avenue Baptist Church. This church was friendly to Shepherds, and one of its members was on the Shepherds board. This man's sister-in-law was a resident of Shepherds, and his mother-in-law was a member of this church. There is much agriculture in this section of the country. Our friend raised bees and was in the pollination business. While visiting and presenting Shepherds at this church, we wanted to visit a couple who had prayed for and supported Shepherds for many years.

Arriving at their home, we had a wonderful visit, at which time we thanked them for their love for Shepherds and all their monetary gifts. The woman's mother, aged 92, lived with them. We engaged her in our conversation also and were surprised and delighted to hear this sharp nonagenarian. She had a special hobby which intrigued us greatly. She quoted verses from the Bible beginning with each letter of the alphabet. At her age, we were impressed by how sharp she was. It was noteworthy how she made a chore that was difficult for some, very easy by using the alphabet to quote and memorize Scripture.

God blessed us along the way by meeting people like this. The Psalmist said this: ***Your word I have hidden in my heart that I might not sin against you.*** (Psalm 119:11)

NATIONAL BISON RANGE

L eaving our campsite near Kalispell, Montana, we headed south through the vast open spaces of Great Sky Country. Our goal this Sunday morning was Dixon, Montana, a small community along highway 200. We arrived in Dixon early at the Community Baptist Church, and soon the pastor arrived. I unloaded our things from the truck, and Margie helped set up the display. I also prepared the projector for the presentation during the services.

BISON RANGE—MONTANA

There were few in Sunday School, but more came for the morning service. Pastor Jim Herd and his wife Caren served in this church. We knew his dad in Oregon, but this was the first time to meet Jim. I showed a Power Point in Sunday School and preached during the morning service.

After church, the folks served lunch to all, and we had a wonderful time. These little churches were an inspiration to us. Shepherds Home has friends all over who faithfully pray and support them when they can. This is encouraging.

Pastor Herd knew we would be going right through the National Bison Range, so he and his wife were kind to guide us in their car as we followed to the entrance of the Park. The open areas are immense, and one could easily get lost if they did not know where to go.

The National Bison Range website states that *President Theodore Roosevelt established the National Bison Range on May 23, 1908 when he signed legislation authorizing funds to purchase suitable land for the conservation of bison.* This range covers some 19,000 acres of natural grassland, and approximately 500 American bison roam this vast area. They share it with other interesting animals as well. Elk, mule deer, bighorn sheep, and black bear also live on this refuge, along with over 200 bird species. A well-marked loop took us through the extent of the range. Ordinarily it takes several hours to do this. Because we did not want the darkness to overtake us in a very unfamiliar place, we went through quickly. A drive through this marvelous attraction is well worth the time spent. The views were spectacular, and we had many opportunities to see these grand animals up close, which made the trip worthwhile. Visitors receive warnings how to act as they visit this marvelous place. Strict rules for behavior are posted, and explicit instructions about what is not acceptable. Only the wise know how important it is to follow such warnings.

To see a herd of bison grazing on this beautiful mountain slope was a site we will never forget. I call it God's handiwork in nature. To think our loving heavenly Father created the bison and many more animals for our use and enjoyment is amazing. I am grateful for this, and I trust you will thank Him for all He has given us. ***For by Him all things were created that are in heaven and that are on earth, visible and invisible, whether thrones or dominions or principalities or powers. All things were created through Him and for Him.*** (Colossians 1:16)

BOMBAY BEACH

BOMBAY BEACH—CALFORNIA

It took a long time to make contact with anyone in this part of the Imperial and Coachella valleys of California. After repeated phone calls and e-mails, we had located the pastor of the Baptist church and set a meeting date. We parked in El Centro, California, and left in plenty of time to find the place and get set up for the service.

This was new territory for us, and the drive along the Salton Sea was quite an experience. The dank smell of salt filled the air. Things were very arid, and we travelled many miles before seeing any hopes of getting to our destination. Finally, we saw the entrance with a sign reading, "Welcome to Bombay Beach." Records indicate this was once a very prosperous community, but now it appeared depressed. The Salton Sea is 223 feet below sea level, making it the lowest spot in California.

We found the church, met the pastor, and set up for our meeting. We had wondered if anyone would come, but were happily surprised with a good attendance. We learned during the evening that a resort on the opposite side of the highway leading to Bombay Beach had people attending the service that night. Had we known this earlier, we would have scheduled a meeting at this place, also.

The believers in this church were very receptive to the Shepherds ministry, and we admired the retired Army officer who was pastor. He had lost his wife and was doing the ministry alone. I believe his mother lived in this community also. On a practical point, we know this was a difficult work, but we were so glad this pastor plugged away preaching the gospel to the needy souls in this depressed community. Certainly, his reward will be great for faithfully shepherding this church. ***Moreover, it is required in stewards that one be found faithful.*** (1 Corinthians 4:2)

BUTTE CANYON

━━━━━━━◆━━━━━━━

Forrest Ranch Baptist church in California invited us to talk about Shepherds. The place we parked our trailer was several miles up the road from the church. We arrived and set up according to instructions, then met the couple, owners of this property. It was especially nice, because they had a full hook-up for our trailer. This was an added blessing. Most places had electricity and water but no place to dump the waste tanks.

While we were parked at this lovely wooded area, the owners invited us to have a meal at their home. We walked from our trailer to the house. Built overlooking the canyon, this house was impressive. I suppose that is the reason they call this area Canyon Butte. This huge ravine filled with magnificent trees was beautiful.

As we neared the house, we looked at the large chimney, which appeared to be several stories high. The fireplace inside the house was enormous. The house was not small, but well-built and cared-for. We could tell that to maintain this house and property one would keep very busy. The grounds also required much work to keep them tidy.

It was an enjoyable experience to be guests at this couple's lovely place overlooking the canyon. Can you imagine how beautiful the sunsets were? For a future day, Isaiah prophesied a beautiful scene: *"For you shall go out with joy, and be led out with peace; the mountains and the hills shall break forth into singing before you, and all the trees of the field shall clap their hands."* (Isaiah 55:12)

CAN WE MAKE IT OVER THE PASS?

M any trips for Shepherds presented challenges. We traveled this stretch of highway between Medford, Oregon, and Redding, California, with much prayer. In Medford, while filling up at the gas station, we heard there were unsettling weather conditions, especially in the Siskiyou range in California. Before our trips, we always requested prayer, and each day before beginning our journey, we prayed. At this point, we certainly needed the Lord's help for the next leg of this journey.

When a threatening storm approached, it was useless to begin a trip over such a questionable route. By the time we reached Grants Pass, Oregon, the reports were more encouraging. At one more point, we would check to see how things were ahead of us on Interstate I-5.

We stopped in Ashland, Oregon, the real starting point of our route over the mountains and to the city of Redding, California. There, the word was more encouraging, but still we were doubtful about this trip. Should we get a motel and wait it out, or try it and see what happened?

We prayed, and continued onward toward the Siskiyou Range. As we got closer to the questionable stretch of highway, things looked better, and we were encouraged. On the final miles to the summit, we were met with a surprise we did not expect. There was a cloud clearing, and as we made the ascent, we noticed that the road was bare. This was wintertime, and normally there was a lot of snow in this part of the country. Pretty soon we were on pavement that was not wet, and there was not much snow on the sides of the road. What was going on?

I became concerned, because we no longer had to use the heater in our truck. Could something be wrong with the engine? The dashboard gauges did not warn us that anything was wrong with the motor. Soon I decided to open the truck window. We did not use the air conditioner while climbing, so as not to put an extra strain on the motor. Here we were in the winter on a road that normally had snow. The road was bare and dry, the sun was shining, and we were traveling with the windows open because it was so hot. We even used sunglasses for that trip.

This is one of those stories hard to believe, but certainly enjoyable for us. All we did was thank the Lord for all the dear people who prayed for us on these trips. It was an obvious answer to prayer. How grateful we were for prayer warriors who faithfully remembered us on our trips. God is good, and His Word encourages us to ***Pray without ceasing.*** (I Thessalonians 5:17)

CAN YOU TOP THIS?

❖

T hings happened along the way we wish might have ended differently. We were in Gardena, California, parked at the Calvary Baptist Tabernacle. Pastor Jim Solomon and wife Sharon were so kind to us, allowing us to use a parking place for our trailer. Behind the church was a huge parking lot, which at the time they leased to the Toyota Company for storing their vehicles.

DAMAGED TRAILER ROOF

We had just arrived, and Pastor Jim was helping us park our rig by directing us into the shade of a huge tree just behind the church. All was going well until I felt a low muffled rumble and a slowing of the truck and trailer as I backed it into its place. With all the noise coming from the most travelled freeway in California, Highway 405, I guessed the rumble I heard was normal.

We parked at this spot for several weeks, travelling out from there to many churches in the greater Los Angeles area plus several places much beyond that big city. When our meetings in that area terminated, we moved to Fremont, California, to our good friend Pastor David Einer and his wife Leela at the Berean Baptist church. At the rear of this church, also, there was a huge parking lot and even a dump station. What a treat for us! Ordinarily we had to find a dump station every 7 days to drain the trailer tanks. This always involved a major move every week. We had our routine, and it usually all went well. Margie did all the inside preparations while I got the outside matters done.

For some reason I looked at the roof of the fifth wheel trailer because of the incident mentioned at the first of this story. When I climbed the ladder to look at things and give a general inspection, I was shocked at what I saw. Apparently, a low hanging limb had scraped the top of the trailer and gouged it out severely. Immediately I consulted with members of the church about a place in their town where I could take the trailer for an evaluation. A kind member knew exactly who I should talk to and in fact requested the company to send an inspector to our parked trailer and appraise the damage. He came and measured the torn coating and roofing material, and returned to his office to calculate the cost of repair. Shortly thereafter, he called us with the bitter truth. To repair the roof damage would cost several thousands of dollars. In fact, it was going to be many thousands of dollars. Margie and I felt we just could not do this. On the other hand, this terrible gouged and damaged section of the roof would doubtless bring much grief when we encountered heavy rains.

I took the trailer to the company and explained that we just could not pay the unbelievable high price they were asking. I requested a lesser repair job, which I knew would not fall on sympathetic ears. HOWEVER, the owner's son heard our conversation, and his father asked him to do the work on our rig. He examined it and came back to tell me that he repairs these things all the time, and he would fix it. He also assured me it would be well done and roadworthy. We cannot tell you how relieved we were to hear this good news.

A couple of days later, he called to say he had repaired the roof and we could come and get the trailer. We did, and when we got the bill, we were more amazed than words can tell. He had done a masterful job fixing this gaping trench in such a beautiful way that it was remarkable. The price was right also and very reasonable compared to the original estimate. Margie and I could only praise the Lord for such a wonderful answer to prayer. The Apostle Paul's words mean more than just financial things, but what a truth is contained in this treasured verse: ***Now to Him who is able to do exceedingly abundantly above all that we ask or think, according to the power that works in us, to Him be glory in the church by Christ Jesus to all generations, forever and ever. Amen.*** (Ephesians 3:20-21)

A NOSTALGIC VISIT IN PRESCOTT

W hile we ministered at the Open Door Baptist Church in Prescott, Arizona, a friend from Glendale, Arizona, offered to take us to some sites we would enjoy. This kind lady loved to drive and seemed to know all sorts of places of interest. We had a meal with her and some friends at the IHOP Pancake House. We then headed out of town several miles, and this is where the fun began. A large sign pointed the way to Prescott Pines. This was a Baptist campsite where I had spent a lot of time during my younger years.

PRESCOTT PINES CAMP—ARIZONA

As we drove into camp from the access road, memories filled my mind. Stopping at the camp dining room, I remembered how I had zealously served my tables during family and adult camps. I was amazed by the huge amount of tips I received the last night of camp. All the coffee cups had a stack of coins and bills under them. That was a lot of money for a teenager working his way to camp. Then we walked from the dining room to the chapel. Memories filled my heart of the times we had special speakers. I recall Dr. William Pettingill, one of the contributing editors of the Scofield Reference Bible, and former dean of the Philadelphia School of the Bible. Not only did I get to hear his fabulous teaching, but I also received another honor. During free times at camp, they chose me to drive Dr. Pettingill to Prescott, Arizona, to do some shopping. What a privilege this was! This stately man enjoyed walking around town, using a cane. He bought a few things for himself and his wife. I will never forget that experience.

As we walked around the camp later, I tried to find a couple of rocks under which I had hidden some loose change years ago. I did not find them, because camp improvements took them away. The well that furnished cool, delightful water to the camp was a significant part of life around the grounds. I remember looking down the well's huge opening and seeing the timbers that secured the walls. As a youth, I looked in there one day and saw a huge diamondback rattlesnake resting on one of the timbers.

Because I was in on some of the initial camp construction as a young person, I had "privileges" when camp was not in session. A lake nearby was a favorite swimming hole for some. One day when my friends were swimming, we had close encounters with some dangerous water snakes. I thought it best not to go there again, and I am not sure it was okay for people to swim there.

In the early days, tents were set up on nice wood platforms, which made them a very good place to sleep. Afternoons were quite hot as the sun heated the dark canvas. It was a blessing that each tent had electricity and a single light bulb. The camp caretaker was a friend. Eventually he left that position, and an interesting thing happened. My brother Ernie, after his term in the service, received his discharge from the Navy and became caretaker of the camp. Now we had a vital connection with Prescott Pines. When my grandfather Robins died, I went to live with my grandmother. During the summer months, I took her to camp, and though inexperienced, I built a nice base for the tent she purchased, and I also screened the little front porch so she could enjoy the scenery and be free from mosquitoes. She really enjoyed this.

The day we revisited the camp was very special to me. Margie had never seen the site, so I was glad she could see where I had spent some of my summers as a youth. About two years after the lady from Glendale took us to this camp, she became ill, and finally cancer took her life a few years later.

How precious it was to meet friends along the way as we traveled. They became part of us, and we cherish those wonderful memories. I am so glad that godly parents and grandparents had instilled in me biblical principles as a youth. Surely, Solomon urged the youth in his book about this: ***Remember now your Creator in the days of your youth, Before the difficult days come, And the years draw near when you say, "I have no pleasure in them":*** (Ecclesiastes 12:1)

CARBONITE TO THE RESCUE

———————◆———————

We arrived at our motel in Fife, Washington, where we headquartered while ministering at the Southside Baptist Church missionary conference in Tacoma, Washington. I had prepared a Power Point presentation to show at the conference about the Shepherds ministry. We were excited about this church, because we had a long relationship with them as missionaries and afterwards as Shepherds representatives. Pastor Ron Hill welcomed us warmly as we went early to set up for the conference.

Before leaving for the conference, I quickly reviewed my Power Point on the laptop to make any adjustments or corrections. To my utter dismay, when I plugged the thumb drive to the computer, it opened, but it was not the right program. I never know how these glitches occur, but when they do, it leaves us desperate for an answer. It is always good to pray about all these things, and we did.

I know the Lord made me think about *Carbonite*. The purpose of this company is backing up files. However, I must admit I had never tapped their resources, even though I subscribed to their service. At this critical hour, I made my first attempt to recover files from this company that backed up our files on their central computers. Being a novice, I had to go slowly and read all the fine print as I went online. I logged in to their company, typing my user name and the password I had created when I opened the account.

What a blessing to see the file I wanted on the screen! With a few clicks of the mouse, I was able to download this Power Point presentation to my computer and put it on a thumb drive. What a relief! That night they did things differently at the conference. They moved three separate groups into the main sanctuary, where we showed our Shepherds presentation three times.

We thought the conference was very good, and those attending were most gracious in their comments about the Shepherds ministry. What a blessing to represent an organization that ministers to individuals with developmental disabilities. We never ceased to be amazed how receptive people were to this special ministry. The verse which is central at Shepherds in all their presentations is this: ***"I will set up shepherds over them who will feed them; and they shall fear no more, nor be dismayed, nor shall they be lacking,"*** ***says the LORD***. (Jeremiah 23:4)

A PUZZLING STORY

———————◆———————

It was always interesting to go to our daughter's unit at Shepherds and visit with the women. Joy usually sat by herself, because she was totally deaf and never spoke a word. She was, however, extremely curious, like her dad, so she knew pretty well what was going on.

At Shepherds, they provided all the recreation and fun activities that most families offer their children. In Joy's unit, we watched with interest as the ladies put together puzzles. Like anyone, they would pick a piece, glance at it, and then search for its home in the puzzle. Soon we learned that they were very good at this, and it was intriguing to watch the picture taking shape before our eyes.

They would sit for long periods working on puzzles. We never did figure out how they chose the puzzles. There were all kinds of pictures: mountain scenes, rivers, children playing, favorite person puzzles, etc. About anything your heart desired, they had a puzzle. One of the counselors said they were able to work these puzzles even if they could not see the picture.

One day I entered the room where the big table was that contained all the puzzles. The women were busy doing a puzzle. I looked closer and noticed that the puzzle pieces were face-side down. The ladies looked at the table, and the puzzle part they had already solved. Then they picked up a piece, and examined it. After studying and looking at the piece in their hand, they would soon find the spot where it fit. We concluded that these master puzzle solvers had the ability to determine very quickly where each piece belonged. We stood in amazement as they completed the *faceless* puzzle so quickly. A verse from Solomon comes to mind as I see these dear women work at puzzles. ***Whatever your hand finds to do, do it with your might; for there is no work or device or knowledge or wisdom in the grave where you are going.*** (Ecclesiastes 9:10) I hope we are all as eager to do the Lord's work as they were to do their puzzles.

A SURPRISE ENCOUNTER AT CHURCH

W e had attempted many times to schedule a meeting in a church in Holtville, California. For some reason, we had trouble making phone contact. Finally, we succeeded, and while we were in El Centro, California, we drove to the *carrot capital of the desert.*

When we went to a new church, we never knew what or who we would meet. The preliminary set-up procedure was very important, and that's the reason we always arrived early at the church. With our literature table in place and details worked out with the audiovisual director, we were ready. In this church, we were not invited to present the ministry in Sunday School, but attended their adult class. It was always nice to study the Bible no matter who the teacher was. As soon as the class was over, we headed for the main auditorium to meet the pastor.

He outlined what he wanted us to do, and the service began. The pastor was very kind in his presentation of us and Shepherds. We had never met before, but it was obvious that he was acquainted with the work. We gave a quick overview of the ministry and highlighted the literature table, encouraging folks to help themselves to any material they could use. We also, at an appropriate time, circulated clipboards soliciting names and addresses of those who would like to receive next year's calendar. We almost always had a very good response to this part of the service.

That morning in the message I gave a short update of our daughter Joy. Included in this was a brief account of our years in Brazil as missionaries. The focus of my message was always an appeal to pray for and support the ministry of Shepherds. When the service was over, we made our way to the literature table so we could answer questions and suggest the appropriate material according to the desires of those who were perusing the display.

At one point, as people were exiting the building, a person spoke to me in Portuguese, which really surprised me. It was delightful having this interchange in the language we had spoken for many years. To our surprise, one after another came by the table, speaking Portuguese. It was because we mentioned Brazil in our message that they felt free to use their native tongue as they left the service. What a wonderful time we had for a few minutes! The Brazilians told us there were quite a few attending the services there. They were **snowbirds** taking advantage of the warmer climate in Holtville. The pastor later confirmed they came each winter to escape the cold weather in other parts of America where they lived. Besides the wonderful reception at this church and their support for Shepherds, we were blessed by the presence of these Brazilians who appreciated hearing about Shepherds. What a joy it was to greet these people, reminding us of Paul's word to the Philippian church: ***Greet every saint in Christ Jesus.*** (Philippians 4:21)

A VISIT TO A HUTTERITE COLONY

◈

W hile we were visiting and ministering in Cut Bank, Montana, a friend told us about the Hutterite colonies. We arranged a time to travel a short distance out of town to visit one. After checking into the colony, an easy procedure, we were given a guide to take us around and introduce us to this place. Our tour-guide was a delightful young woman dressed in her typical Hutterite apparel. She was very articulate and showed a real interest in informing us of the customs and ways of her heritage.

HUTTERITE COLONY CHILDREN—MONTANA

Boys and girls played in the schoolyard dressed in their beautifully hand-made clothes. The boys wore full suits with all the frills. The girls also in their long dresses were attractive. German is the language spoken in the colony. We discovered that all whom we encountered were bi-lingual, being fluent in German and English. English was the language used in school, but elsewhere the German influence was evident.

The impressive part of this visit was the high degree of organization displayed in everything they do. It almost seemed that the clock was the general manager of the organization. Each person had his schedule of responsibilities, and a clock alarm rang to announce the next chore.

Out in the fields, men and women worked to prepare, maintain, and harvest each crop. Others would process the products in whatever way was appropriate for each item. Some perishables were stored in cold rooms; the prepared foods were in a deep freeze. These storage places were immaculately clean, and the vegetables grown were show-pieces. We never saw a bigger cabbage than in the colony. They were enormous. We saw vats of aging sauerkraut and many other things wonderfully prepared for market or their own use in the colony. They gave us some items to take with us as a reminder of their special ways to prepare food. They also gave us a hand-made broom, like ones you can buy in the store. They are all made right there. A visit to the cobbler shop was revealing. Everyone's shoes are made in the colony. You can say the colony is self-sufficient.

The chicken production aspect of the colony was impressive. We saw huge chicken coops or barns. Each step of the chicken-raising process was highly organized, even to the special areas in which the hens laid their eggs. Everything seemed to be automated to a degree, with each Hutterite busy with his or her responsibility.

To describe each process in this highly organized colony would take too much space. A good encyclopedia will give you information about these interesting people. We attended a chapel period while there, and the students walked into the chapel in an orderly manner and sat in their assigned seats. Singing and reading of the Bible followed. We enjoyed seeing this part of their communal life.

To our surprise, we were invited into some homes in what I describe as a longhouse, only much nicer. As each couple marries, they attach their new home to the last one in the row. Their homes are well constructed and identical. The material used in construction is top-grade, and the workmanship is excellent. They are two-story, and I think that families live together in this way. Perhaps mom and dad live on the main floor and the children upstairs. We had delightful visits with some of the residents and were impressed with their kindness and cordial ways. Paul may have been talking about a business meeting in the church, but I believe we can apply this to way the Hutterites go about their business. ***Let all things be done decently and in order.*** (1Corinthians 14:40)

A SPECIAL AUDIENCE

---◆---

We discovered years ago, when missionaries to Brazil, that speaking to the residents at Shepherds was a privilege. In the early years, they were all children, like our daughter Joy. When I spoke to them, they responded to questions I asked and were like a group of junior boys and girls. They were energetic, curious, responsive, and certainly well behaved. They learned many of these qualities through the excellent teaching and guidance by their Shepherds leaders.

Years later, when I was a representative for Shepherds, the chapel leader asked me to speak. I was delighted to explain to the residents how I told churches about Shepherds. I opened God's Word and gave them spiritual truths. We were always impressed how the residents responded to spiritual teaching. During chapel, we were thrilled to hear them sing. Some had the gift of singing on tune; others were at different levels on the scale. Their enthusiasm made it a joyous occasion, and we loved it. When it comes to prayer, we were impressed by how these dear ones talk to God. It is real to them as they express their heartfelt love for Him and their earnest intercession for others. Indeed, the Shepherds residents are very special, and King David's words remind me of them. *Give unto the LORD the glory due to His name; Worship the LORD in the beauty of holiness.* (Psalm 29:2)

A STRANGE EXPERIENCE WHILE IN PALO CEDRO

———◆———

When we presented the Shepherd's ministry at a Baptist church in Redding, California, we were guests of a very thoughtful couple who lived in Palo Cedro, California. Their guesthouse was very comfortable, and we spent special moments in the area and appreciated their hospitality.

Our story does not involve them, but a phone call from our son. One night Rawlie called saying he was in our home in Ferndale, Washington, on one of their many trips to the city where his wife Gina's parents lived. While in our house, the phone rang and a man whose mother lived in the next street up called to ask where we were. Rawlie explained we were on a ministry trip for Shepherds in California. This man wanted our help, because his mother had just died.

We were able to make contact with him later that night, and he told us of his mother's sudden death. It was all so fresh, but he did want me to have the service. I told him we were on our way home after the next meeting and would be there to work with him about details.

In the meanwhile, I called the deceased woman's sister, a dear friend, who lived next door. The phone rang a long time, and finally she answered. It was obvious she had been sleeping and wondered who would call that hour of the night.

I naturally thought she was involved with all the confusion going on next-door, the paramedics, etc. I gave her our condolences, and she was confused. She told me later that she was upset that I called her so late at night. She knew nothing about her sister's passing. She had missed all the noise of sirens, etc., and even her nephew's persistent doorbell ringing to tell her what had happened.

We had never been in such a situation. Our son called telling us of our friend's death and her son's desire to talk with us. I called the deceased's sister to express our sympathy for the loss of her sister, but she knew nothing about it. What a story! And to think she lived next door to her sister.

When we got back to Ferndale, we had the memorial service, and all the pieces of this amazing story came together. In life, we need to be ready for anything that comes our way, and there are many unknowns. James said it best: ***Whereas you do not know what will happen tomorrow.*** (James 4:14) Are you ready in case your life ends today? Trust Jesus Christ as your Savior and be ready.

A SURPRISE AT
THE END OF THE SERVICE

O ur ministry with Shepherds afforded us untold blessings as we visited churches. We parked in El Centro and
moved out from there on Sundays to the towns on the road
to Los Angeles. We had never been to this church before but
had made numerous calls seeking permission to come some
day and tell the folks about Shepherds.

Finally, the day came, and we made the hour or so trip
westward to our pre-arranged meeting. After setting up, as
we did at every church, we attended the Sunday school class
taught by one of the churchmen. During the morning service, we presented the work of the Home, telling interesting
things as we talked about Shepherds. Because we spoke in
different churches each week, I usually spoke on the same
passage of Scripture. I learned that each week the Word
spoke to hearts in different ways, and I was always encouraged. Telling moving stories of Shepherds residents "rang a
bell" with churches, and it was encouraging to see how God
spoke to hearts. That motivated us to keep on preaching the
Word and watching the Lord do His work.

This particular day, at the conclusion of the service, the
pastor really appreciated the report about Shepherds. He
urged the folks to ask the Lord what He would have them

give to this ministry. Then he asked if there were any questions from the audience. Some asked questions or remarked about what they heard. At one point, a man at the rear of the church stood up and started what turned out to be quite a talk on working with those with developmental disabilities. Apparently, he was involved in one of these services but was very impressed by what Shepherds was doing. He compared Shepherds' ministries with what he saw locally in the services provided by his city. He was praising Shepherds highly for the integrity of their services, and he made a plea to the church people that morning. He urged them to support this ministry, and was very forceful in his appeal.

The pastor called the ushers, took an offering, and finished with a passionate word of prayer to close the service. As we dismantled the display table, took down our projection stand and projector, and started packing things into the truck, the pastor came to us with a check. We were overwhelmed with the very large sum of money they gave Shepherds that morning. The preacher and the other man's appeal had challenged the folks to give generously. We praised the Lord for the privilege He gave us to be in this church and share again the wonderful story of Shepherds. All we can think of is Solomon's words of long ago: ***The generous soul will be made rich, and he who waters will also be watered himself***. (Proverbs 11:25) We praise the Lord for those dear Christians.

A TURN DOWN THE WRONG ROAD

M argie received an invitation to speak to the women of the First Baptist church of Pinole, California. We had presented Shepherds in this church previously and were kindly received by Pastor Baker and his wife. The church was enthusiastic about the ministry of Shepherds, and Margie now had the opportunity to share more with the women.

The trip from Fremont was only about an hour away, so the travel was easy. While Margie enjoyed her times with the church women, I went to pastor Baker's home for fellowship. It was nice visiting with him and becoming better acquainted with his history as a pastor in our fellowship. I enjoyed a snack at the pastor's house, and after a while returned to the church to wait for Margie. That night, Margie shared the program with some others involved in various ministries and said the time was very profitable.

After gathering her things and saying goodbyes, we started our journey back to Fremont. By this time, darkness prevailed, and we relied heavily on the GPS machine our son had given us for Christmas. Traveling in the general area of Oakland and San Francisco has its challenges. Things were going smoothly, and I turned in the direction I thought we should be going. In just seconds, I realized I was on an unknown road, and it did not look good. The freeway was wide with many lanes, and yet I saw no cars. I wondered how such an immense road would be "carless." Then, to my horror, a traffic sign appeared indicating San Francisco ahead. I realized I was on the entrance to the Oakland Bay Bridge. I knew in an instant that once I entered those lanes indicated by the sign, our trip to Fremont was going to take a long time.

I asked the Lord for wisdom and guidance. I looked way over to my left, and there seemed to be a return lane to get back where we started this episode. I was taking a chance to cross so many lanes to my left, but I was desperate. We were also apparently alone, and only the Lord could have kept the traffic out of those lanes. We were apparently by ourselves on this freeway. I knew it was the Lord who showed me how to return on that special lane. I have no remembrance of ever seeing anything like this lane that I could access and go back to where we started. I was fearful that a patrol officer would see this wild maneuver and pull me over. However, the Lord worked this out by allowing only us on that huge freeway entrance. We will never forget this miracle.

Escaping this nightmare trip to San Francisco, we stopped at the next corner store and got a snack for our trip home. I could not believe what had just transpired and how good the Lord was in helping me resolve the problem. We made it home, and all I could do was meditate on the verse that has been my comfort for years: ***The LORD preserves the simple; I was brought low, and He saved me.*** (Psalm 116:6). I am eminently qualified to fit the description of this verse. Praise the Lord.

AFTER ALL THESE YEARS

The world is relatively small. We went to Lakeport, California, to tell about Shepherds. Ray Smith was pastor of the Baptist church there. His dad was the director of the Natal, Brazil, seminary where Margie and I worked a few years earlier. Now we were visiting their son's church. What a privilege! They treated us royally, and Mrs. Smith even knew how to make Brazilian coffee. What a treat!

This story gets more interesting. When we were students at Biola College in Los Angeles, years ago, our colleague Gordy Wilcox also studied there. He lived in Lakeport. Without our knowing anything about his work, we discovered he and his wife have a home for those with developmental difficulties. While in Lakeport, we visited Gordy and his wife and learned more about their ministry with these dear people. Each Sunday these residents attend church, and It was such a pleasure having them in the service when we presented Shepherds.

Little did we know that one day this side of Heaven, we would meet Gordy again. He had been very ill, and we were so thankful we were able to see him and meet his wife and the residents of his home. The Lord must have special blessings for them as they have this wonderful ministry. When Paul wrote to the Romans these words: (Romans 1:11) *For I long to see you, that I may impart to you some spiritual gift,*

so that you may be established, he certainly did want to be with them. What blessings God gave us in being with friends.

ADJUSTING GRAVITY ON A BICYCLE SEAT

W orking for Shepherds brought us a multitude of special happenings that we will never forget. In the town of Polson, Montana, while parked at the First Baptist Church, we became friends with many of God's chosen people.

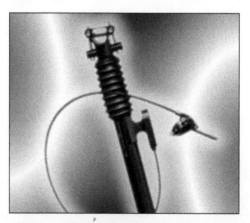

GRAVITY DROPPER SEAT

In the Polson church, we met Arlen and Miriam Wisseman. He was an interesting man with God-given talents that were remarkable. He had suffered an auto accident that almost took his life. We met him years after this, and he and his wife invited Margie and me to their home for a meal. In itself, his house was a marvel to behold. He showed us the special battery room where huge batteries stored electricity via the help of his elaborate solar panels. In an emergency, his house had electricity. These things were very interesting to us.

Then Arlen took us to an additional building at the side of his house, and we could hear machines making a fair amount of noise. He proceeded to show us a simple looking item. It was a bicycle seat post that he called Gravity Dropper. I did not understand this. For bicyclists, this is a well-known subject. When you ride downhill, it is very handy and advisable to have the bike seat at a lower level. This gives the rider more control. When you are on level ground or going up a hill, an elevated seat gives you more control and provides more power as you pump the bike. This may not be the most professional explanation, but in "round numbers," that is how I describe it. Arlen invented this gadget, and he made different kinds -- each for a specific need by bicyclists. He showed us the machines and the whole process of how he made them at home. I did not want to miss this adventure. God has especially gifted this man to invent such a process, and the product is world famous. An Internet search for Gravity Dropper will prove what I am saying. He sells them all over the world.

One more thing happened before we left Polson. Arlen invited us and another couple to his place to do some "plinking". I can best describe this as "an informal target shooting done at a non-standard target". My wife knows I am not good with a rifle, and my Amazon experience trying to kill a pig was proof. Now we are here at Arlen's doing plinking. A machine shot targets into the air, and we tried to hit them. To my surprise, I actually did hit some. That will doubtless be the only time I will ever do that, but it was fun while it lasted. Friends such as Arlen and his wife are a rich heritage. *A man who has friends must himself be friendly, but there is a friend who sticks closer than a brother.* (Proverbs 18:24)

[Check out the website for more details - http://gravity-dropper.com/products/]

PACKING IN A SNOW STORM

S ometimes we felt like relaxing instead of packing our trailer. However, our schedules in California demanded we prepare for departure from Ferndale, Washington. It was snowing hard, and the snow accumulation was getting us nervous about pulling our trailer from its parking place to the street in front of our house. I called our good friend Lloyd McCarty, a truck driver, who came and put chains on our truck. It was quite a job. He had previously offered to do this, and I appreciated his kindness. We did not realize that Lloyd was not feeling well. He also helped us get the trailer out of the yard and onto the street. That was a relief, because there is an incline from the trailer parking space alongside our house, to the street. With much prayer and determination, we made it out of the yard. I wanted Lloyd to drive it out, but he insisted I do it because I knew our truck better.

We continued loading the trailer, and finally started our long journey to California. Even though we had chains for one set of trailer tires, we never had to put them on. We live on **Swede Hill** in Ferndale, and there was more snow here than downtown Ferndale. In some areas of our travel, there were accumulations of snow, but road crews kept the roads clear. When we got to the Portland area, things changed. Apparently, the snow had been so fierce that snowplows could not keep up with the demand. The result was a pavement so rough that it was almost impossible to travel more than 25 miles per hour pulling the trailer. The snow had fallen on the highway, and because the plows could not remove it fast enough, the cars had dug trenches in it. Then to complicate things, the temperature dropped lower and froze all those humps and bumps into solid masses over which we had to travel. We went for many miles at a very slow speed. We had to do this to keep things in the trailer intact. We did not want to have a chaotic situation with cupboards opening and a disaster in the trailer. It is hard to describe how bumpy that ride was on the ice-encrusted state highway. We were very glad when things returned to normal.

Finally, the road cleared and we had an easier trip. We always looked forward to warmer climates when we left our home in Ferndale. That night we made it to Salem, Oregon, where we stayed in our favorite campsite. We were so thankful to get that far without incident. Sleep was sweet that night, knowing we were on our way to our destination. Look at the end of this verse which talks about sleep. ***It is vain for you to rise up early, To sit up late, To eat the bread of sorrows; For so He gives His beloved sleep.*** (Psalm 127:2)

PICTURE TAKING

A s missionaries, we learned to take pictures. We may not have learned to take good pictures, but at least we chronicled our ministry with pictures. I came on it naturally because my father was a photographer at one time and took pictures all his life. I wished he could have been alive during the digital era of photography, as he would have enjoyed it so much.

In the early days, I took pictures of all the churches where we ministered. I also included a picture of the pastor and his wife. However, these two things are only a tip of the iceberg in my hobby of taking pictures.

Margie and I walked each morning for exercise. Our goal every day was to walk a mile. On these walks, we encountered innumerable things to photograph. For years I have always carried a small camera in my pocket. In fact, one time at a church in Santa Maria, California, I was taking a picture of Pastor Carl Wheeler and his wife Florence, and he jokingly said, "Don't break the camera!" As it turned out, I snapped the picture and yes, it was the last picture that camera took--it broke! Today we still laugh about it. I ordered another one that day, and soon we were back in business.

FLOWERS ON MORNING WALKS

Now, getting back to those early morning walks. The variety of plants and flowers we encountered were spectacular. God's handiwork in nature has always intrigued me. I even have a section in my Bible classes with that title. I give all kinds of examples of God's creative genius. I have done it for years, and the classes love it. The beautiful things we capture on film are such a blessing. Someday I must categorize them. To print them in a book is too expensive, so I will just enjoy them at the computer.

Taking pictures was not limited to our morning walks. As we traveled along, we encountered such amazing views that I determined I would try to get them in digital format, also. Because I am not a professional, this works for me. As I drive, I can hold the camera focused on the windshield or side window, and take shots. You may ask about the reflection from the glass. Now with the magic of software, I discovered ways to get around that. I have been able to achieve some amazing views -- most taken through windows.

I also enjoy taking pictures of people. I have taken many photos of couples, and insist on editing them by blacking out the background, and with another computer program, bringing the couple closer together. Normally these shots look as professional as a photo shop would do it. This is not because I am good at it, but because of the fantastic software available.

I think Isaiah was the first one who even hinted at something close to photography. He described the way folks years ago would paint the outline of Jerusalem in the palm of their hands so it would remind them of home when they were away. Who knows, maybe it was like a tattoo. The Lord has US inscribed on His hands. *See, I have inscribed you on the palms of My hands; Your walls are continually before Me.* (Isaiah 49:16)

PILLOW-ADDICTION

---◆---

Sometimes we humans get ourselves into some situations that are hard to figure out. My neck has never been very cooperative at sleep-time, and I usually have trouble finding a comfortable position.

Now we move ahead to our trip to Shepherds for the yearly meeting with representatives and the Shepherds staff. We always looked forward to this because it was such a big help in our ministry. Another great plus was the fact that we could see our daughter Joy for a few days. We left Ferndale and drove to Seattle, where we stayed in a motel. We left early by air the next morning for Union Grove, Wisconsin, the home of Shepherds.

That night in the motel, I had a rude awakening when I discovered, to my dismay, I had not packed my neck pillow. This was way out of character for me, but I did it, and I spent a miserable night. I have never slept on airplanes or any other transportation. Arriving in Milwaukee, Al Pick kindly met us. On the twenty-five mile trip to Shepherds, I asked Al if he would stop at a Walgreen's drug store so I could get a pillow. He kindly accommodated my request and near Union Grove found a Walgreens, and I purchased my pillow. The reason I chose Walgreens was that I had recently purchased one there that worked, so I figured they would have one at another Walgreens, and they did.

So, our stay in Union Grove went well, because I had a pillow that was compatible with my peculiar neck problem. I had not realized how accustomed I was to an item like this. Sleep is a God-given thing. I often refer to this verse: ***It is vain for you to rise up early, To sit up late, To eat the bread of sorrows; For so He gives His beloved sleep.*** (Psalm 127:2) Thank God for the sleep He gives us.

REMINDER OF FORMER DAYS

———————◆———————

In our travels for Shepherds, we were always thrilled with the intriguing experiences God allowed to happen in our lives.

At the Sleater Kinney Road Baptist Church in Olympia, Washington, we had friends who knew about Shepherds. In addition, the pastor (Paul Pierce) was formerly in a church south of his present church. The Lord allowed us, by His grace, to have a part in this pastor's spiritual journey, for which we are still thankful.

First, we were invited to speak to the Sunday School at this church. They were interested in the history of Shepherds. We showed pictures, spoke, and had a table with literature and things of interest in the church foyer. Folks freely took the literature, and many asked about other things they wanted to know.

During the Sunday School hour, we were very surprised when a couple visiting from the east stood up and identified themselves. They made the most interesting comment we had heard in a long time. They were present at Garfield Avenue Baptist church in Milwaukee, Wisconsin, when that class decided to start a special class for the developmentally disabled boys and girls. They went on to say how the class eventually started Shepherds.

It was so special for Margie and me to meet members of that class and visit with them. The story of Shepherds is a thriller, and just to see God's hand in the formation and development of this ministry was a blessing. We have heard from different ones who gave us bits and pieces of the story. Each one gave us more information that helped as we represented the Home in churches.

Although spoken for a different reason, Isaiah's words here express our sentiments about this incident in our lives with respect to Shepherds: ***"Remember the former things of old, For I am God, and there is no other; I am God, and there is none like Me."*** (Isaiah 46:9)

REPAIRING A NEW FIFTH WHEEL

The trip from Ferndale, Washington, to El Centro, California, was uneventful except for several sections of very rough road. When we packed our trailer for travel, we had to be careful to have things secured so they did not fall and break. No matter how many precautions we took, something was bound to happen. Some miracles always seemed to be evident as we traveled. Normally we secured television sets with special devices sold by RV supply stores. We did not have any problem with that, and we never had to tie it down. The small edge molding on the shelf kept it from sliding off. Another miracle was our espresso maker. Not a very big machine, but we had it sitting on top of that special non-slip material sold just for this purpose. Miraculously, it never moved nor fell in all the miles we traveled those many years.

Arriving in El Centro at Pastor Sanchez's home where we usually parked our trailer, we were horrified to find the interior of our trailer covered with most of the contents from one cupboard slide-out. What a mess! About the time we discovered this, Pastor Chavez appeared at the trailer door. We invited him in, and he immediately saw the problem. Graciously, he offered to install a special fastener that would eliminate further problems with this slide-out. While we were away getting some supplies, he fixed the cupboard.

From then on, we never had it happen again. We affectionately referred to that latch as ***Albert Sanchez.***

Several times on our trips, I had to purchase and install special hardware that would keep the drawers closed. They were tricky to work on because of the hardware position and the small area in which we had to work. Ironically, I installed special openers on the swing-up type doors, which are located above eye level, around the inside of the trailer. Without them, you could not keep them open and put things inside easily. With special cylinder closers, all you did was lightly pull down on the handle to close the door. Pastor Sanchez helped me with several other practical things to make living in our trailer easier. Paul told the Galatian Christians something that reminds me of this fine pastor: ***For you, brethren, have been called to liberty; only do not use liberty as an opportunity for the flesh, but through love serve one another.*** (Galatians 5:13)

ROAD KILL AT ITS BEST

---◆---

One of our routes to Montana was via the main road going north from Coeur d'Alene, Idaho. A good distance up this highway is the town of Sagle, Idaho. We had the privilege of visiting this church twice in our years with Shepherds. They were very receptive to our presentation, and we always were welcome there. We met such special people in churches, and this church was no exception. Pastor David Hess and his wife pastored here.

We had a very nice place to park our rig, out of the flow of traffic at the rear of the church. It was on a lower level and accessed from the rear of the church lot. We got settled and set up with electricity and water, and as usual enjoyed our short stay at the church.

It is interesting how you associate certain things with churches and pastors. One day we were talking to Pastor and Mrs. Hess at their home where we were guests for lunch. I pulled my Parker pen out to jot down something. The pen did not write very well, and I complained. Pastor Hess immediately informed me that the best ballpoint pen we could own is a Zebra, and it never fails. At the next town, I found one, and he was right. It is the best pen we have owned.

Another interesting thing happened while at this church. They gave us the keys to the church so we could use the facilities as needed. By the kitchen in the fellowship hall/dining room, was a small chest-like freezer just like one we had in the Amazon. One day the pastor told me that we were welcome to help ourselves to the meat in this chest.

ROAD KILL MEAT

We took him up on this offer, and I went to the chest, where I read the instructions printed plainly on top. We were welcome to take anything from the chest, but had to give our name, the number of packages and the date of removal. The pastor explained that his church had an agreement with the Highway Patrol or the Idaho Fish and Game Department. Road-kill, which is prevalent in these areas with heavy deer populations, is something they take care of. The responsible department grants institutions and churches the privilege of dispensing this meat. It is processed, quick-frozen, and given to those who will help them distribute it. What a blessing to take a couple packages of deer burger. It was delicious and a wonderful provision for us while on the road. How unique and special for the individual states to have this service! Instead of wasting tons of meat, they give it to those who appreciate and use it. This reminds us of Paul's words spoken for another subject but in part applicable to what we experienced in Idaho: ***Command*** *those who are rich in this present age not to be haughty, nor to trust in uncertain riches but in the living God, who gives us richly all things to enjoy.* (1 Timothy 6:17)

SAY "CHEESE"

O ur visits to Union Grove, Wisconsin, and Shepherds were
always the highlight of our years. As a representative,
I learned more each time how to represent this wonderful
place when visiting churches. To meet other representatives was also a tremendous blessing for us. Last, and very
important, was the privilege of seeing our daughter Joy again.

We often wondered if Joy really knew us, but each time
the staff assured us she did. Several indications were always
there, but it was good to hear it from those who were with her.

Both Margie and I attended many business sessions.
Some were not as necessary for Margie to attend, so she
would spend time with Joy.

As the end of the week drew near, we knew that our
custom of taking cheese products to our family and friends
was upon us, and we must get to the store. The retail shop
was small but had just about anything you could desire in the
cheese line. It was fun being in this store and choosing items
to take back to Washington.

Back at Shepherds, we put the cheese in the small refrigerator in our room. The day we left for home, we packed
carefully all the suitcases and carry-on items. Each piece of
cheese we placed in double plastic sacks and packed them
in the suitcases with plenty of insulation around them. They
would be cool in the luggage compartment of the plane. We

always breathed a sigh of relief when all the items were safely home with us. It was fun giving them to family and friends. ***And remember the words of the Lord Jesus, that He said, 'It is more blessed to give than to receive.'***(Acts 20:35)

ROBIN'S NEST

As we traveled, many things happened along the way. We ministered for Shepherds at the Sterling Baptist Church in Sterling, Alaska. This town is unassuming and located a long distance from Anchorage. We were on our way home after the meeting, and an attractive ice cream shop called Robin's Nest caught our eyes. It looked almost new as we entered. The atmosphere was cheery and gave one the sensation of stepping back in time. Some of us remember the ice cream shops that were rustic and very old fashioned. This one was like them, but with a modern touch.

ROBIN'S NEST RESTAURANT—ALASKA

The reason this name caught our attention was because my grandparents' home in Phoenix, Arizona, built by my grandfather, Joseph Robin, had the same name. Grandmother and Grandfather Robin always called their home the Robin's Nest. My granddad, during a gospel invitation at Eastside Baptist Church, in Phoenix, Arizona, had come to where I was sitting. He looked my way as the pastor was speaking and drew me to Jesus. I became a Christian that day after his kind invitation. Now you can appreciate why this sign in Sterling, Alaska, captivated our attention as we drove by.

I wish I could remember the facts about this ice cream shop as it relates to robins. Somehow, robins were involved in a distinct way that prompted the owners to call it the Robin Nest. It seems they kept flying to this spot and it was obviously a subtle sign to the owners what they should name the shop. Well, the sandwiches and ice cream we got that day were a treat as we drove back to Anchorage. The Lord is so good in giving us precious memories like this along the way.

Paul talks about believers being able to appreciate and enjoy the things God makes available as we live from day to day. ***Command those who are rich in this present age not to be haughty, nor to trust in uncertain riches, but in the living God, who gives us richly all things to enjoy.*** (1 Timothy 6:17) Imagine that: He even gave us a Robin's Nest.

RUTH BOSE

For many years that our daughter Joy was at Shepherds, so was Ruth. We became friends on our visits to see Joy when we were home from Brazil. We realized very soon that this fine woman loved the residents and was actively engaged in their care. Ruth invited us for lunch many times at a local restaurant in Union Grove and insisted Joy come too. What a gracious person! It was not easy taking Joy out, because it was difficult for her to walk and she sometimes choked while eating. We reciprocated and invited Ruth for lunch several times, as we enjoyed her friendship.

RUTH BOSE

One time we had Joy come out to Washington State, and Ruth was visiting her daughter who lives in the same state. She did the magnanimous gesture of bringing Joy and taking her back to Shepherds. Her kindness was beyond the line of duty and always done with a smile.

Ruth's love for Joy was manifest in so many ways. At the hospital one time, Joy was obviously upset with the new surroundings, and the hospital staff was uncertain they could deal with her properly. Ruth, with grace and expertise, used some sign language and then placed a magazine by Joy, indicating she would return. Joy loved magazines and calmed down instantly.

When Joy's residency at Shepherds ended, we boldly asked Ruth if she would be willing to accompany Joy and bring her to her new facility in Lynden, Washington. Typically, Ruth agreed and accompanied Joy on her last earthly journey, before taking her heavenly trip, just 6 months later. Ruth stayed extra days to instruct the staff regarding the idiosyncrasies of Joy's care and how better to communicate with her.

When Shepherds could no longer keep Joy because of their inability to provide the care needed as she aged, we spent weeks trying to find a place that would accept her. Later, Ruth told Margie that if we had not found a place to care for Joy's needs, she personally would have cared for her. We know she really meant this and are eternally grateful for such a person who loves the developmentally challenged and proves it by her actions. Her daily presence and ministry on Shepherds campus will never be forgotten when she retires.

For this and a myriad of other reasons, Ruth has been a precious part of our family these many years. Her dedication, love, patience, and energy have endeared her to many others besides ourselves. Our hearts fill with gratitude for the years she has labored at Shepherds and touched so many lives. Jesus said something significant about Mary in the Bible: ***She has done a good work for Me.*** (Mark 14:6) Ruth is a beautiful example of *good works* as she has served the Lord and Shepherds.

SAFETY FIRST

———◆———

We learned a long time ago as missionaries to Brazil, that when you are traveling and presenting your ministry in churches, you have to think SAFETY all the time.

Arriving at a church in Encinitas, California, we were soon set up except for the power cord to the electric outlet source. The pastor showed us where to plug in, and we put down the power cord. These sections of cord are about the size of one's thumb. The outlet was inside the church, just behind one of the entrance doors. I trailed the electric cord right along the wall next to the sidewalk. When I crossed over to the trailer, I always tried to find a joint in the sidewalk and lay the cord in it, so it would be less dangerous. However, that does not solve the problem of safety. I also carried bright yellow duct tape, which was highly visible, and securely fastened the cord to the sidewalk with it. One problem, however, is, that at night yellow turns black.Sometimes I was able to place the cord suspended in air, high above the crowds, thereby eliminating the possibility of stumbling on the cord. You see, we do not do these things just to make it all look nice. We must be very careful to prevent injuries due to the power cord tripping someone. Therefore, we always did our best to keep it as safe as possible.

Inside the church, we had the same challenges with all the cords needed for our equipment. Generally, I used the yellow duct tape to keep cords neat and covered so no one would trip. Proverbs says it best for us. ***Then you will walk safely in your way, And your foot will not stumble.*** (Proverbs 3:23)

SAVED BY A SPARK

S ummertime in Arizona is HOT! We were parked at the rear of a church, and the accommodations were nice. We had water and a place nearby to dump our tanks when necessary. We were parked on a cement slab and so did not have the discomfort of sand and dirt as in some places.

In our fifth wheel, we always used evaporative coolers, even though the unit was equipped with an air conditioner. We opted for this because Margie got along much better with moist air than with the dry from an air conditioner. Another advantage was that coolers only draw about as much electricity as a light bulb. Therefore, we could have cool air in warm weather when we used the Honda generator, which was too small to run an air conditioner.

WHERE THE SPARKS FLEW

This particular night the wind was blowing gently, but it was hot air. It was nighttime, and as was my custom, I went outside to check things to see if all was okay. As I descended the trailer steps, God ordered what happened next. We parked quite close to the rear of the church. Large air conditioner units were along that side of the church. The outside church light was on, but being a small bulb, it did not illumine much. As I descended the steps, my eyes glanced at an unusual sight. I saw, in the darkness against the church wall, a spark that kept arcing repeatedly. Alarmed, I used my cell phone and called the pastor of the church, telling him the unusual sight. He thanked me.

Not long after this, he appeared, and shortly after that, an electrician whom he had called. Immediately they turned off the breaker that supplied current to our trailer. Now the church and we were in the dark. The electrician examined the situation and came up with a verdict of what had happened. Years previously, when they installed the electrical system for the air conditioners, the electricians had used one of the pipes through which the electrical wires ran. Also, and I am not an electrician so cannot speak intelligently about this, they used the actual pipe as the neutral for the electrical process. As I understand, this is not permissible and a violation of the proper installation of the system. The electrician was quite aghast at what he discovered. There were probably four large air conditioners running on this system. He said that our alarm over seeing the spark saved the church a major disaster. He said the whole system could have blown up and caused a major fire.

Next day, Sunday, at church the pastor explained very carefully the situation to the church family, expressing his gratitude for our being there at just the right time to see this and report it. God's timing is always right, and He is so good. We never question God's perfect leading in our lives. How true is His Word and the comfort of this Scripture verse: ***And*** *we know that all things work together for good to those who love God, to those who are the called according to His purpose.* (Romans 8:28)

SAVING POSTAGE

There is always a need for correspondence in any organization. When we started our ministry with Shepherds, the orientation classes were very interesting and informative. I knew right away we were going to keep the Post Office very busy. Many reports were required to maintain a semblance of order as we worked in the churches.

One of the normal Sunday activities in the churches was passing around clipboards so people who desired a Shepherds calendar could sign up and receive them. These sheets had spaces for names, addresses and email addresses. In some churches, the pastors wanted to give the announcement about signing up for the calendar.

But I am ahead of my story. While at Shepherds getting this orientation about sending in all these reports, an idea clicked in my mind. As we were leaving, after a week at Shepherds, I mentioned to the secretary that I would be sending her the sign-up sheets and other things, but perhaps differently than she normally received them. I casually said, "Just wait for the next email", and we left for Ferndale.

After our first meeting in California, we had a sizable number of sign-up sheets from this church. Now was the time to put in practice what I had decided to do about reporting. The sign-up sheets with diverse colors of ink, even though we had attached a nice ballpoint pen to each clipboard, were to

237

be sent to Shepherds. But sending a raft of papers is expensive. That's why my new plan went into effect immediately. I scanned each page carefully and in high resolution so the secretaries could easily read them. Problem solved. When they arrived via email as attachments, the secretaries could either read them online, or print them and transfer the information to their system. As far as I know, we may have been some of the first to do it this way. I say this because I asked some of the representatives and they sent theirs via U.S. Postal Service. An added note: all the other records I did this same way, by sending them as digital attachments. This way when we were far from a post office or did not even know where one was, it made no difference, because we sent them all via cyber space. What fun! When I read Paul's letters, this verse speaks volumes to all of us in this present age that have the luxury of email and easy communication. ***See with what large letters I have written to you with my own hand!*** (Galatians 6:11) Imagine the person who carried this letter. What a difference we have today, with many ways to communicate.

TECHNICAL SUPPORT
WHEN UNEXPECTED

———◆———

We had a super place at the side of the church to park our trailer at Montana Avenue Baptist Church in Caldwell, Idaho, for our Shepherds meetings. While there, we also travelled to other nearby churches conducting meetings for Shepherds. During the day, I spent most of my time contacting churches for future meetings. We were very grateful for cell phone coverage in most places we traveled.

Shepherds checked out a nice Dell laptop computer which we used constantly for email and for keeping records of our Shepherds meetings. One day I got the shock of my life while I was working on the laptop. It stopped, dead, never to run again. I contacted the person at Shepherds responsible for our equipment while on the road, and he told me to call a number with the information given me over the phone.

I secretly thought that maybe in the big cities, Dell would send someone to help me, but there was no way Dell was going to send someone to Caldwell, Idaho. I made a call, and technical support at Dell was superb. They had things under control, and that was obvious. The dispatcher instructed me to make another call, which I did, and a date and time were set for the encounter. To my surprise, the technician came right to our parked trailer way out here in little Caldwell,

Idaho. Imagine this, a man finding our trailer and knocking at our door. He came in, sat at the computer desk, and soon had extracted the old hard drive and installed a new one. He asked me to sign some papers, and then he left. What a wonderful deal! We were so thankful that Shepherds does their work in a business-like manner. They had the proper warranties and insurance for occasions such as this. I thanked the Dell technician for his promptness and efficiency. Even though Paul was referring to the way churches should conduct business, the same applies to Christian organizations, like Shepherds. I am so glad they followed this principle. ***Let all things be done decently and in order.*** (1 Corinthians 14:40)

NEED FOR A NEW INVERTER

S everal of our stories originated in Gardena, California, because we could park our trailer for longer periods there. Some ministry churches gave us this privilege, and we deeply appreciated it.

On one occasion, we left the fifth wheel trailer at the Tabernacle Baptist Church in this city and traveled to our home in Ferndale, Washington. We asked a favor of the pastor to look in on our refrigerator now and then just to make sure it was working ok. One cannot be too careful about these things.

When we got back to California after a short break at home, we entered the RV and sensed that not all was well. Apparently, about the time we arrived in Gardenia, the RV inverter "decided" to stop functioning. We had never had this experience before, so it was new to us. In fact, we asked Pastor Solomon what he thought the problem might be. He immediately said we should check the inverter. I hardly knew where it was located. Finally, with his help, I could find it, and the job of taking it out was colossal. It was in a very awkward position in the RV, and to access the bolts that secured it to the floor was a challenge. Once the inverter was out, I had a church member test it, and the result was negative. Now we had to find a place that could order one for us. With a suggestion from Pastor Solomon, I found the place and ordered it.

In a few days, it arrived, and then the process of mounting it in the trailer began. Admittedly, it was a hard job. Pastor Solomon was recovering from an illness that had taken its toll on his health. I did not dare ask him to help. Typically, though, Pastor Solomon is always ready to help others. He, in his weakened condition, insisted on doing the work. After we mounted and turned the inverter electricity on, we praised the Lord, because we had an RV whose electrical system functioned normally again. This inverter keeps all the electrical needs of the trailer and machines regulated properly. It was a huge relief to have it working again, and we thanked Pastor for his gracious help. The inverter for the trailer was, physically, as the Spirit of God is for the believer, spiritually. Do you remember the words of Luke in Acts 1:8? ***But you shall receive power when the Holy Spirit has come upon you; and you shall be witnesses to Me in Jerusalem, and in all Judea and Samaria, and to the end of the earth."*** It is only after a person receives Jesus Christ as personal Savior that he is born again and has God's power in him.

MAGIC OF MESA

ome things were puzzling to us as we traveled from state to state for Shepherds. However, there was not a dull moment, because interesting things happened all along the way. We called for a meeting in Mesa, Arizona, and Calvary Baptist Church invited us.

At first, the pastor wanted us to have an evening service, and we were content with this. Toward the end of the week, I received a call from him saying he was not feeling well, and would I have Sunday school and the morning service. What a blessing to hear, not that he was ill, but that we would have a larger hearing for Shepherds.

The pastor's father, Roger Williams, was a friend of Dr. Andrew Wood, the founder of Shepherds. Roger, Jr., was the pastor, and we enjoyed him very much along his wife and family. Because we parked on the church facility, things were much easier for us. The only negative, but one we faced almost all the time, was dumping the trailer waste tanks weekly.

We learned something very interesting while in Mesa. Several of our Ferndale, Washington, friends visited and spent part of their winter there. We even spent time with a dear friend from Kalispell, Montana. We called this the magic of Mesa. There is something about Mesa, Arizona, that is intriguing.

So from time to time, we were delighted to make contact with friends and enjoy a meal together. We learned updates about other friends in Ferndale and things going on in our home church there. To encounter close friends so far from home was indeed a blessing we did not expect. One time friends we had met while in Anchorage representing Shepherds came to Apache Junction. We met for supper at a restaurant and had a great time recounting our memories of Anchorage. These are blessings we never took for granted. ***A man who has friends must himself be friendly, but there is a friend who sticks closer than a brother.*** (Proverbs 18:24) There is more to this verse than just the words. One thing is sure: to have friends is a gift from God.

MAY I SIT WITH YOU?

C hapel time at Shepherds was always special. The logistics of getting all the residents there, finding their seats, and quieting down for the service, was routine. However, we enjoyed watching it happen. For the regular caregivers it must have been monotonous, but not for us.

Our daughter Joy was always the last to enter, because she was a gawker and had to make sure everyone was there first, before she would enter. She looked everywhere and wanted to know what was going on in every room.

As chapel time drew near, there were always the last minute situations that required help from the caregivers. One time when we were seating Joy at the rear of the auditorium, a resident approached me and asked a touching question. "Mr. Poulson, where are you going to sit?" I assured him we would be sitting next to Joy, our daughter. Then he asked an interesting question, "May I sit with you"? We felt honored, and tears welled up in my eyes. This fine man, whose singing voice had blessed many, chose to sit with us. As chapel progressed, it was noteworthy that he said "Amen" or "that's right" as the pastor was speaking.

The more we knew the Shepherds residents, the more we loved them. They taught us so much as they sang with great enthusiasm. They quoted Scripture with diligence and answered Bible questions with conviction. God rewards acts of kindness and service done to those who love the Lord as doing it unto Him. "And the King will answer and say to them, ***'Assuredly, I say to you, inasmuch as you did it to one of the least of these My brethren, you did it to Me.*** (Matthew 25:40)

SHEPHERDS CHAPEL

MEETING A FORMER CLASSMATE

W e did not do a good job of keeping up with our BIOLA classmates. Through the years, we had limited contact with some, but it seems that in time we lost contact. One such person, who had years before visited us in Ferndale, was Helen Nagle. She and her husband stopped by Ferndale on one of their trips, and we had a meal together at a local restaurant. Helen has always been very interested in Shepherds, and she and Margie talked periodically on the phone.

While we were at Calvary Baptist Tabernacle in Gardena, California, we decided to visit Helen, who lived in the Fullerton, California, area. We traveled several freeways in our pickup truck, and with GPS's help, found the Morning Side Retirement Center in that city. At Helen's apartment, we enjoyed some time visiting with her. She had invited us for lunch, but we did not expect to see what we witnessed that lovely afternoon.

A walk around the grounds was a delight. The landscaping was spectacular with all the flowers in full bloom. When it was time for lunch, we approached the dining room and looked down on it from the floor where Helen's apartment was. It was quite a sight! The tables were perfectly set with white tablecloths, a floral centerpiece, and all the trimmings fit for elegant dining. We sat at a pre-selected table with Helen and received menus from which we had our choice of several things for our meal. The food was delicious and the fellowship very special. While eating, Helen pointed out notable residents sitting around different tables. We were impressed with the caliber of residents in this retirement center. Helen mentioned a certain woman, and it so happened that her father had been a professor at BIOLA COLLEGE. In fact, Dr. McCullough was my Greek professor. He was a godly man whom we respected and admired. Several others were also outstanding missionaries and Christian workers, now retired, living their lives in this very special facility.

Helen is a faithful prayer warrior, and we appreciate so much her ministry of support and prayer. What a privilege it was to visit her that day! Helen is an example of Paul's admonition about prayer. ***Be anxious for nothing, but in everything by prayer and supplication, with thanksgiving, let your requests be made known to God.*** (Philippians 4:6) We thank God for Helen Nagle.

MIRACLE HEARING DEVICE

Years ago, we met Mr. and Mrs. Eschol Owenby in Tucson, Arizona. He owned an audio business and offered to help Brazilians by furnishing special hearing equipment to those who needed it.

The end of that story is beautiful. We did take some devices to Brazil and fitted Luzia with one. This enabled her to enjoy family and friends much better and hear sermons at church with ease. We were thrilled with this gracious gift from the Owenbys.

In our travels for Shepherds, little did we even dream of meeting this lovely couple again. What a surprise to see them at a church where we were presenting the ministry of Shepherds! Mr. Owenby invited Margie and me to have lunch with them at a local restaurant that week. We met them and had a wonderful time recounting the good old days when we first met. They were thrilled to hear about Mrs. Luzia's use of the hearing aids and how she enjoyed being able to hear friends and also her pastor's messages, etc. Margie had taught this dear woman in her seventies to read her own language—Portuguese. She expressed to Margie that her prayer was to be able to read the Bible through before her death. The Lord granted her wish, and she read it more than once before her home-going.

At another time in Tucson, Mr. Owenby invited us for a picnic at one of the scenic desert monuments near his town. Mrs. Owenby was unable to be with us, as she was quite frail and not feeling well. Mr. Owenby took charge, fixed a picnic lunch with all the trimmings, and drove us to this interesting place. At lunchtime, we chose a nice picnic table and enjoyed our meal in the desert setting.

Months have passed quickly, and Mrs. Owenby had someone contact us requesting we phone her in Tucson. We did and were saddened by the news that her husband had recently passed away. We were sorry to hear this and called her subsequently to visit over the phone. She is at home, and has good help.

We reflect on these special moments so much. What a joy this couple brought us. We miss Eschol and his gentle, generous ways and are so thankful for the opportunity to have known him. God programs people into our lives in such a variety of ways. We trust you are grateful for your friends and the privilege of praying for them and enjoying their friendship and fellowship. Paul did this with his friends in Philippi. *I thank my God upon every remembrance of you*. (Philippians 1:3)

"I'M BEE ZEE"

A lmost all residents at Shepherds worked in some way, and that helped with their monthly tuition costs. It was a pleasure to tour the campus and see the great variety of work done by the residents. One particular department, Shepherds Enterprises, was dedicated to this. They made and packaged many things. We noticed how dedicated the residents were to their work. Some did more than others. There was an opportunity for most to do useful work, for which they received compensation. We noticed they had a serious attitude toward their work and did it with a sense of pride.

We were surprised that even the lower functioning residents had work. They folded paper towels, sorted silverware, and shredded paper. Our daughter was involved in the latter. A counselor worked with her to accomplish this. A specially adapted paper shredder made it safe for her. Joy would be encouraged to feed a piece of paper into a slot, and it appeared she caught on to this fairly well. However, I must admit they rewarded her with an M & M or a cookie. This was her encouragement to continue. We were impressed how Shepherds residents did these jobs.

Also, we remember a man whose job was to keep the coffee and tea supplies ready for mealtimes. He took his work very seriously, and he did his job well.

The title of today's story comes from one of the men who was working in the hallway at Shepherds when we passed by. We wanted to engage him in conversation, but he had no time for small talk. When we tried to talk to him, he responded forcefully "I'm ***bee zee***". After all these years, we still laugh about how he answered us. The apostle Paul instructed the Thessalonians about their work ethic this way: ***For even when we were with you, we commanded you this: If anyone will not work, neither shall he eat.*** (2 Thessalonians 3:10). We are thankful for the good training these people received at this Christ-honoring ministry.

INSPIRATION FROM A
SENIOR PASTOR

This story begins long ago when I visited Ferndale, Washington, and the First Baptist Church. I was there because of a girl who would eventually be my wife. I wanted to meet her folks and the people with whom she fellowshipped. I was so impressed with the friendliness of this church, and the dedicated pastor, that in 1952 I decided to become a member.

PASTOR CARL WHEELER

After our years as missionaries, and eighteen years as pastor of this church, we began our ministry on the road for Shepherds Baptist Ministries. Our itinerary took us to Grover Beach, California, where Pastor Carl Wheeler, our pastor from Ferndale, was now retired and living with his daughter and son-in-law, Joanne and Joe Campbell.

We had a meeting for Shepherds in the church he was attending. The pastor gave permission to park our rig on church property, which was very nice for us. Pastor Wheeler came to visit us in our fifth wheel trailer almost every day, and what precious moments they were for us. He had recently lost his dear wife of over 70 years. Pastor Wheeler was never old in his thinking. He was on the cutting edge of current events and kept himself well informed with political and religious goings-on.

On a given Sunday, we were able to attend this church again, but this time Pastor Carl Wheeler was speaking. The regular pastor was away on a much-needed vacation, and the board asked him to speak. This Sunday was very special for Margie and me. We had the privilege of listening to Carl Wheeler preach. Not only did he preach, but he also had communion service. How could a man his age do all this? Well, it is not over. There was a baby dedication, which he also conducted that morning. Margie and I were overwhelmed to hear this godly pastor preach, do communion, and conduct a baby dedication. Why were we impressed? Carl Wheeler at that time was 96 years old. For us, that morning was amazing. It was a blessing to hear this seasoned pastor preach the Word. What a blessing! The Psalmist said it best: ***They shall still bear fruit in old age; They shall be fresh and flourishing.*** (Psalm 92:14)

IT DOESN'T HAPPEN VERY OFTEN – HEAT VS. COLD

When two boys in a family are missionaries and the other lives in Anchorage, Alaska, the chance of being together is slim. In 2007, we were in Gardenia, California, holding meetings in various churches. Through correspondence with my brother Ernie, we learned that he and his wife were coming for a mini furlough to visit a few churches and tend to other issues while in the States.

We received their arrival date, and Margie and I drove to the L.A. airport to meet them. Ernie and Verda's granddaughter Esther was also there. She had a truck, but we expected to transport some of them in our car to Upland, California, where they would stay at the Church of the Open-Door guest home. The reunion was great. Ernie, Verda, and Siang (their goddaughter), could get into Esther's truck, so she took them to Upland, and we returned to Gardenia. At another time we drove to Upland, about 41 miles from Gardenia, and enjoyed a great meal and visit with our family. Later while they were here, we had returned to Ferndale, our home, and Ernie, Verda, and Siang flew to Bellingham, Washington, seven miles south of Ferndale. My younger brother, Harold, arrived from Anchorage, and again we had a wonderful time together. It was rare to get all three brothers together. We cherished those moments.

HAROLD, ERNIE, AND RALPH (LAST PICTURE TOGETHER)

Something interesting happened while my two brothers were in our home in Ferndale. Ernie has lived in Singapore for over 62 years. It is hot there, and they use air conditioning most of the year. My Anchorage brother lives in cold country, Alaska, and seldom has warm weather. Here is where the story gets interesting. Ernie, the oldest of the brothers, has trouble keeping warm when in the States, because Singapore is hot all the time. On the other hand, Harold is warm-blooded and seldom feels it cool enough for comfort. The day we all three were in our house was interesting. It was slightly cool at that time of the year, so Ernie was COLD. However, Harold was too hot. We had the furnace on for Ernie, but a strong fan directed on Harold. It kept them both happy and was hilarious. It may be out of context, and these certainly were not my neighbors, but we really did want to please my brothers. ***Let each of us please his neighbor for his good, leading to edification.*** (Romans 15:2)

JUST PUT IT IN THE MIDDLE OF THE STREET

FIRST BAPTIST CHURCH DUCOR, CA

Off highway 99 in central California, there is a town called Ducor. This town is very small and did not have much going on when we drove to the First Baptist Church. This is hot country, but thankfully, we had a very nice place to park and a full hook-up, which is always much appreciated.

A rewarding part of our ministry was meeting wonderful people associated with the churches. The pastor showed us our parking place, and we discussed plans for the Sunday ministry. During our morning presentation of the Shepherds ministry, the folks were very receptive. I preached during the worship hour and gave a Power Point presentation in the evening service. One thing that impressed us about these folks was their generosity. At the close of one of the services, a man gave us some honey, which he processed on his farm. It was very good.

The next day, by previous arrangement, the president of Shepherds, Dr. William Amstutz, and his wife, Nancy, met us in another town at Denny's, about 17 miles from Ducor, in the town of Delano. This was an encounter which we would never have dreamed possible. Dr. and Mrs. Amstutz were on Shepherds business in the Bakersfield area and asked if we could meet them. So, we decided on a mutual halfway point. What a privilege to have lunch with this fine couple. We cherished these special times.

The church in Ducor was not new. It was an old building but very nice. They had obviously taken good care of it through the years. The pastor told us this most unusual story. Years ago, the church was built on the corner of two streets. It became evident they needed more room in the church to carry on their ministries. It was not practical, at that time, to add on to the church or to make a separate facility to accommodate their needs.

After much debating, and we are sure many business meetings, they decided to make a basement in the church. This, of course, was a major undertaking. How were they going to do that? Some ingenious architects came up with a solution that is not ordinary, but it worked. With the proper equipment and work force, they lifted the church with jacks. Then with gentle care and expertise, they moved it to the center of the street that ran along one side of the church. With the church safely and securely now sitting in the middle of the street, they left it for a long time. They excavated the basement area, laid the foundations, properly placed the partitions, and plumbed for the kitchen and bathrooms. Then the big day arrived. They raised the church building from its temporary spot in the middle of the street and placed it carefully on the new basement foundation walls. After the interior of the basement was properly finished, painted, and furnished, they had a dedication service. What a day that was! Can you imagine a city now that would allow a church building to sit in the middle of a street for months? This project was one of the most unusual we saw while traveling. Jesus talked about good foundations: *He is like a man building a house, who dug deep and laid the foundation on the rock. And when the flood arose, the stream beat vehemently against that house, and could not shake it, for it was founded on the rock.* (Luke 6:48)

KEEP LOOKING UP, BUT
WATCH YOUR STEP

———◆———

All the years we represented Shepherds, Margie and I walked a mile or more each morning before breakfast. It was a good time to get out and get our daily exercise. Most of the pictures I took during those years were done while walking. Amazing things took place as we walked the streets and blocks of all the cities we visited.

Each morning In Fremont, California, we met a woman sitting at the street level of the sidewalk leading to her home. She was beautifully dressed and perhaps of East Indian descent. She was pleasant, and we looked forward to seeing her every day. Each time we passed her, she pointed to her wrist as if she were wearing a wristwatch, and it was obvious she wanted to know the time. She must have been waiting for a ride, or perhaps walking to the bus stop. Each day she went through the same motions, and we told her the time. She smiled her thanks.

On this same walk in Fremont, we tried to take as many side streets as possible to keep away from the busy traffic. At that time in the morning, many cars had already left their parking places on the street. Others were still there. We encountered a dear Asian man who could not speak English. He was elderly and kept his yard watered and meticulously neat. Each time we saw him, he raised his hands, smiled, and laughed heartily, probably the only greeting he knew. We looked forward to seeing him on each walk.

Down the street from this man's house, we crossed over to the other side, walking between parked cars. Just prior to stepping on the street curbing, I glanced down. It is always good to watch where you are going. As I did this, immediately my eye caught a folded bill lying on the street. I picked it up in one scoop and kept walking. Shortly thereafter, I looked at it, and to my amazement, it was a five-dollar bill. What a nice find! Margie and I found a favorite parking lot in Paradise, California one time, and we were surprised at how many coins we found there. As the title of this article suggests, we should keep looking up. However, for sure we had better watch our step. One never knows what may be around the next corner. To find a five-dollar bill was a blessing, but we thought of the person who lost it. Are you not glad that God supplies our needs in His own way always? ***And my God shall supply all your need according to His riches in glory by Christ Jesus.*** (Philippians 4:19)

KEEPING TRACK OF TRACTS

---◈---

God chose some special people to serve others in this world. At Shepherds, we were blessed to meet one of His choice servants. We heard about a resident who was known for passing out gospel tracts. We wanted to meet him and did so when we visited the campus.

What a delight to hear his story! When he went to the bus stop, he was prepared He was prepared

to give out God's Word everywhere he went. People waiting for the bus received his gift to them, a tract containing a well-written story of what Jesus could do for those who trust Him as personal Savior. When he arrived in a town, he meandered into various stores and presented tracts to some of the shoppers or store clerks.

At sporting events or other community gatherings, he was always ready to hand a tract to someone. When I was in his unit at Shepherds, I was told that in his room he had hundreds, maybe thousands, of tracts stamped and ready to go. He was prepared to give out God's Word everywhere he went.

I admired him, because when he believed in something, he had strong convictions about it. When we get to heaven, maybe the Lord will allow us to know how many people received a tract from this Shepherds resident and trusted Christ as their personal Savior. We were blessed just knowing him. In our conversations with him, we felt his passion for his tract ministry. How appropriate this verse is to this dear man: *Therefore, my beloved brethren, be steadfast, immovable, always abounding in the work of the Lord, knowing that your labor is not in vain in the Lord.* (1 Corinthians 15:58)

LABELS GALORE

In Redding, California, we presented Shepherds at Grace Baptist Church. It was particularly rewarding, because we had worked with pastor Al Franklin's brother, Robert Franklin, on the mission field years ago. His sister, Lonnie Vaughn, also is a good friend of ours and lives in our home town of Ferndale.

Pastor Franklin's church also has a school. We spoke to the students about Shepherds one day when we were there. At the conclusion of the program, some students approached me and said they had some Campbell labels for Shepherds. We were glad to get these, because we made appeals in each meeting for people to save and send these to Shepherds. Through the years, the home has received several vans, which have helped tremendously in transporting the residents to their activities. It takes a LOT of labels to buy a van, that is for sure. Well, after the students told me about the labels, they brought them to us. We waited, and soon four high school students came carrying a huge box of labels.

Margie and I had several hours of work on the labels. We cut, trimmed, categorized, bundled, and took them to the Post Office and sent them off. What a wonderful gift for Shepherds! At the home, Shepherds also employs their own residents to process labels. It is quite fascinating to see how they have it all organized. Through the years, these labels have helped Shepherds with more than just vehicles. Kitchen supplies were some other things received because of this program. In our presentations, we asked people to help Shepherds by saving labels. It is a positive way many people can help. Jesus said this about Mary and her dedication to Him. ***She has done what she could. She has come before-hand to anoint My body for burial.*** **(Mark 14:8**). I am sure the Lord is pleased when we sincerely do what we can for Him.

LEARNING FROM AN ELEVEN-YEAR-OLD BOY

———◆———

In Oregon while ministering for Shepherds, we met a fantastic young man. One day an eleven-year-old approached us. He was a lovable young person, and to talk with him was a pleasure. Because of our experience at Shepherds and elsewhere, we were aware that this boy was developmentally disadvantaged, and we also realized that such folks had so much to teach us. We learned from the dedicated servants at Shepherds never to downplay the intelligence or abilities of their clients. They considered all of them normal.

In the evening, before many people came to the church, I was at our display table, and this young boy approached me with a hug and started talking. I could tell he had a request for me. He soon asked me to give him a question about the Titanic. I pondered for a moment, and about all I could think of was how far out to sea the ship was when it hit the iceberg. I posed the question to him, and then the fun began. I looked at him and saw that he was in deep concentration. In a matter of seconds, he answered me in a beautiful way and gave other pertinent facts. He let me know that he knew facts about the Titanic that I had never heard before. How interesting it was to listen to him give the facts he knew about this famous luxury liner. His dad later told me that he works at Boeing. He said that each morning a van picks up two men that know the entire electrical system of one of the large planes they build in Everett, Washington. They knew it by memory and did not have to use blueprints or schematics. How valuable they were to this company!

Margie and I realized so many times that the human mind is amazing, and God has given some people special abilities to use them in remarkable ways. When it comes to the developmentally disabled, we have witnessed this repeatedly. Once we knew a woman who periodically asked people their birthdates. This may seem unusual, but she was a human perpetual calendar. When she asked me this same question and I told her my birthdate, she immediately responded that I was born on Saturday. How did she know this? Well, she has a mental gift of being like a perpetual calendar. Since working for Shepherds and having our own daughter, Joy, we have met many special people with gifts we admire. All we can do is thank God for the way He bestows special abilities on certain people.

In the medical field, the study of autism is vast, and volumes are written about it and other related conditions. God has certainly brought some of these special people into our lives through the years. We thank Him for the opportunity of knowing them. We are intrigued with the incredible knowledge they have in specific or general fields of study. How comforting to know God is in control. *I will praise You, for I am fearfully and wonderfully made; Marvelous are Your works, And that my soul knows very well.* (Psalm 139:14)

NO SLEEP THAT NIGHT

W hile parked at the U.S. Center for World Mission facility in Pasadena, California, something happened that changed my life permanently. One night I did not sleep, because I spent the night with acute heartburn symptoms, something that I had experienced only occasionally before this time. I did not tell Margie, because she did not sleep well, and to awaken her in the middle of the night would not be good. I tried most of the over-the-counter remedies we had in the trailer for such discomfort, but nothing worked.

First thing the next morning, I told Margie what had happened that night. Immediately she was very concerned, because she is a licensed practical nurse and knew what some of these symptoms indicated. She wanted me to call our host at the Center so he could get me to emergency. She was mainly concerned that my distress was a symptom of heart trouble.

No. 29 HUNTINGTON MEMORIAL—PASADENA

A rt McCleary took us to the large hospital in Pasadena, where they admitted me to emergency after all the red tape was taken care of. They put me through about every test you can imagine, and obviously, I was not in good shape. In the seven hours I spent in there, I received an ultrasound, intravenous help, nitroglycerin, and even morphine. I had a violent vomiting session, which prompted some of this treatment.

We had just ministered at Trinity Baptist Church in Pasadena, and the pastor came to pray with us. He also alerted our pastor, Dave Lunsford, so people would be praying. Praise the Lord, I was released from the hospital with the diagnosis of severe heartburn and acid reflux condition. Our good friend Elaine McCleary picked us up at the hospital and stopped at the pharmacy where we had the prescriptions filled. I later had an appointment with a doctor in Pasadena who gave me medication and prescribed more. This took place in March 2006. Later tests in Bellingham, Washington, confirmed that I had Barrett's Esophagus. This strange phenomenon has stomach cells, which do an excellent job of handling acidic foods, etc., when in the stomach, but in this case, they were also growing in the esophagus. They do not belong there, and are suspect for becoming cancerous. Therefore, that is when my diet changed for the rest of my life, a small price to pay. Yearly tests convinced the doctor that no more would be necessary unless I had a reoccurrence of symptoms. I have not had heartburn again. The Lord is good, and we praise Him that they discovered this problem before my esophagus turned cancerous. David certainly penned a wonderful word when he said this: *I will praise You, for I am fearfully and wonderfully made; Marvelous are Your works, And that my soul knows very well.* (Psalm 139:14) I am grateful for doctors who prescribe the right medications for most of our ills.

NOT A COMPUTER VIRUS

ach year close to Christmas, the representatives would gather at Shepherds for orientation and updates. It was always a delightful time, because we had not only great fellowship but also the opportunity to see our daughter Joy. To visit the campus of this great institution was a privilege we will never forget. To be with the clients at Shepherds was such a treat, and we will always praise the Lord for times spent there. We can remember them as if it were yesterday.

One of the outstanding events of the year was the Christmas banquet where all the employees and staff met for a fun evening of laughter, inspiration and delicious food. A Milwaukee church each year came to the campus and took the caregivers' places, so they could enjoy the fellowship and banquet. It was very thoughtful of this church. It was especially nice for us, because we got to see Art and Joyce Cavey again, as they fellowshipped at this church. As brand new missionaries in Brazil, we used to attend Art's church in Campinas, Sao Paulo, Brazil. What precious memories they brought back to us!

As time grew closer for our return to Washington, we attended the end-of-the-year activities at Shepherds. This particular year, several of the representatives were in the same residence unit, and we enjoyed the time to visit with each other. On a Saturday night, we went to the gym on campus, where there were risers, and on a schedule, different units from the Home came in, filled the risers, and sang Christmas songs. It was so special to see these precious ones eagerly singing Christmas songs. Of course, we had snacks throughout the evening, and we thoroughly enjoyed them.

We returned to our apartment, visited more with some of the representatives, and then retired to our room. Margie complained of discomfort in her abdomen but went to bed. Then it began--repeated trips to the bathroom, and increasingly severe nausea. This continued until I knew we had reached a critical point and needed help. Fortunately, in those days we had a vehicle at our disposal. I made the decision to take her to the hospital. It was now early morning, and I had to ask directions. We found it, about 12 miles from Shepherds in the town of Burlington. I checked Margie into the hospital with a very kind Christian receptionist. She got approval from our medical insurance, and they put Margie in a room. Her condition worsened, and they admitted her immediately to the I.C.U. That started an experience we will never forget. Margie was desperately ill, and I had to get some rest and return to Shepherds. Early the next morning I checked on her, and she was still very ill. I had to cancel our plane reservations, which cost over two hundred dollars. I alerted our home church and the Shepherds folks about our situation and requested prayer.

Finally, she improved and eventually received her discharge from the hospital. I asked the doctor about her condition, and without hesitation, he said she had the Norwalk virus, without ever having been on a cruise ship. The next day, while she was still in the hospital, I found a Laundromat and cleaned every item in our room. I also scrubbed clean the bathroom with disinfectant and tried to leave things as clean and hygienic as possible. What a job! We learned vividly the truth of this Scripture: ***Do not boast about tomorrow, For you do not know what a day may bring forth.*** (Proverbs 27:1)

ON THE LEVEL

Traveling with a fifth wheel trailer has its challenges. It is especially so when you are not experienced. Travel trailer owners have to learn things either the hard way or the natural way. In order for the refrigerator to work properly, things have to be level. Another motivation for a level rig is the bedroom. If your rig is not level in any direction, things just do not feel right when you are trying to sleep. A level trailer certainly "feels" more stable.

It is all a learning process. Each time we parked for the night, I would learn something else about leveling our unit. I started accumulating different size boards. Different lengths and thicknesses were included in the menagerie of things in the back of our pickup. I understand they have modern devices to keep things level, but we still did it the old way. I bought a set of plastic squares that could be stacked and interlocked for more height. These proved to be very helpful in keeping things level.

When one side of the trailer needed leveling a few inches, we selected some planks for the wheels on the other side. A little extra power would move the trailer onto the front part of the board, and then we would slowly back on to the right position on the wood slab. Sometimes it seemed we could never get it right.

We had to learn more about parking a trailer than just leveling it. Stability was also very important. We experimented with several different devices to help stabilize the "swinging effect" of our fifth wheel trailer. One nice item was a three-legged tripod that fit over the king pin of the hitch. This tripod, properly placed and tightened, really helped calm the trailer motion.

SATELLITE DISH STABILITY

One more item that needed leveling on our trip was the satellite dish. This tripod had a level located in the top. We discovered that when the tripod was level, things went much better. There are many satellites in the heavens, and we had to focus on the right one to get our programs. That process was also challenging as it had an up, down, and sideways adjustment also that had be made precisely for it to receive the station. Was it fun setting up after a long day's journey? Sometimes it was. A good start is like a good foundation of which the Bible speaks. *He is like a man building a house, who dug deep and laid the foundation on the rock. And when the flood arose, the stream beat vehemently against that house, and could not shake it, for it was founded on the rock.* (Luke 6:48)

ONLINE SPOUSES

In our ministry for Shepherds, we never knew what we would discover in our pursuit of finding churches that would invite us to present this ministry. We had a wonderful meeting in a church (unnamed) in Arizona. The pastor and his wife were friendly, and even though there was a small attendance, we knew they were being ministered to by this fine couple.

After leaving this area, we heard that this pastor's wife had died. We prayed for him during this difficult time in his life. Later when we were rescheduling meetings in the same area, I called this pastor's number, and a woman answered. I immediately had to use some tact, because I knew his wife had died. However, I curiously wondered who this feminine voice was on the phone. I ignorantly asked if she was the housekeeper or a relative of the pastor. The kind voice on the phone said she was the pastor's wife. It's not unusual for a pastor to remarry; I just hadn't known the details. She went on to tell me they had found each other on a very popular Online program. Unfortunately, we were never able to return to this church, even though they had invited us to come.

The interesting bottom line of this story is when we were in this church for a Shepherd's meeting, a couple invited us to join them for lunch. We had such a wonderful time, and as I often do, I asked them how they met. Their answer was

275

amazing. They met on the same program that later their pastor used to find his wife. We wondered if their influence had helped their pastor seek this method of finding his spouse. We will never know. Even though perhaps an unusual method in finding spouses, we know this program works for thousands. God's Word tells us this: ***He who finds a wife finds a good thing, And obtains favor from the LORD.*** **(Proverbs 18:22)**

FIRST TRIP AFTER SURGERY

My double knee replacement surgery went well. I could have done better in the knee flexion exercises, but pain usually made me stop. Because of my age, they let me stay in the hospital's south campus and do therapy there. It was nice. I improved greatly, and soon was dismissed. Margie drove me daily to therapy, a trip of about 24 miles.

One day I asked the doctor if I could drive our truck. He said, "try it" and if I could use the gas and brake pedals normally, it would be okay to start driving. That day, after Margie drove me home, I stepped into the truck and tried things. Yes, I could depress the gas pedal with no difficulty and do the same to the brake pedal. From that day on, I drove to my therapy sessions.

With my therapy sessions completed at the hospital, it was time to think about traveling. So, with the trailer packed and the truck hooked to it, we headed for our next meeting in El Centro, California. That is a long trip from Ferndale--about 1440 miles. My surgery was in November and our departure date was in January, so you can see it had not been a long time since surgery. With no problems, we set out for our long trip to California. The first night we spent in Salem, Oregon. It had snowed, and the ground had about two inches of snow. Still recovering from surgery, but doing quite well, I needed to get the trailer ready for our night's stay at the campground.

I had a cane, which I rarely used, because the therapist said I really did not need one. However, it was nice to have when walking through snow getting the water, sewer, and electrical connections set. Margie kept urging me to be careful. A fall on the snow-clad, slippery ground was something I did not need. With that trusted cane, I finished the set-up and was glad to be inside our warm trailer.

For the rest of my life, I will always realize that my knees are artificial. Even though there is no pain, I have always *favored* my knees. I have knelt on them only once or twice. This was of my own choosing. I learned through the years to get under the trailer (when necessary) and do most everything else without putting weight on my knees. As I write these lines, I am waiting for my ten-year check-up. Margie noticed in our journal that the orthopedist told me they would be good for at least twenty years; that would make me about 93 years old. That's not bad. Later, when I had my ten-year checkup, the doctor scanned the x-rays of my knees and said, "It looks like I put them in yesterday." We praise the Lord for such a good report.

One more thing which I have done is self-imposed and not ordered by the doctor. I continue the same set of therapy routines the doctor first gave me before surgery in 2003. It keeps my limbs in motion, and I enjoy doing them. My personal conviction is that of Paul, who wrote: ***Or do you not know that your body is the temple of the Holy Spirit who is in you, whom you have from God, and you are not your own?*** (1Corinthians 6:19) I figure I should do my part in taking care of this temple.

FORCED TO GO BACK

---◆---

W e enjoyed our Shepherds meeting at Faith Baptist Church in Strathmore, California. Pastor Worsham and his wife Alfreda entertained us well. It was fun to be with the church family, and they blessed us with their fellowship. One of the church members, a man 92 years old, blessed us as he played his violin. He played it beautifully, and we were very much impressed as we listened to this wonderful music. The church organist also reminded us so much of a friend in Ferndale.

While at the church, we plugged into one of the electrical outlets in the Sunday school complex. Our display table and all were set up in the foyer of the church. The pastor gave us a key so we could remove our things early Monday morning. We were to leave the keys at an appointed place in the church and close the self-locking door.

After a wonderful day with the pastor and his wife, we enjoyed a special evening of church music. They had several instruments, but the violin solo especially blessed us. We slept well that night and awakened early the next morning; we needed to break camp so we could hit the road and make it to the next town for our next meeting. All went well, and soon we were off and on our way.

Why do things happen this way? After traveling for several miles, I realized that I did not leave the keys to the building in the church; they were in my pocket. We had traveled miles from the church, but we had to return these keys. I did not want to mail them, because it would be too risky. We had been on the road for almost an hour and were a long way from the church. We returned to the church, opened the door, and placed the keys in the place the pastor had requested. We clicked the door shut and started our trip over again. We wondered why the delay and return trip were necessary. Only the Lord knows the answer. Maybe an accident ahead would have been our lot; we simply do not know. However, we do know that the servant who sought a wife for his master Abraham's son, Isaac, said this: ***And he said, "Blessed be the LORD God of my master Abraham, who has not forsaken His mercy and His truth toward my master. As for me, being on the way, the LORD led me to the house of my master's brethren."*** (Genesis 24:27) Yes, what a comfort to know God leads even in our delays.

GALLONS OF WATER

Anyone who has used swamp coolers, or evaporative coolers, knows how they operate. I spent my early years in Phoenix, Arizona, where the summers were HOT. I watched my dad and uncle use these to great advantage in very hot weather. My uncle's house was so nice and cool. I loved walking in and feeling that refreshing cool air. Of course he hand-made all his coolers. He was well versed in manufacturing them, and he did it for years.

When my family moved to Phoenix from Miami, Florida, we first stayed with my uncle. He had sleeping quarters on the second floor of the stand-alone building that he used as an apartment during the hot weather. I recall sleeping in his bedroom upstairs. The heat was intense, and my mother would take the bottle she used to dampen clothes for ironing, and sprinkle the beds generously with water. You would think this would ruin them, but it helped us sleep, as the water made them much cooler.

Our Baptist church in Phoenix had a huge fan with blades that were probably close to a yard wide. A semi-circular enclosure housed a nice wall of shredded wood. A pipe with appropriate holes in it dripped water constantly on the wood. The huge fan sucked the hot Phoenix air through these wet pads and greatly cooled our tin-roofed church. It was wonderful!

SWAMP COOLER

When traveling for Shepherds ministries in our fifth-wheel trailer, we had two very welcome evaporative coolers. One cooled the bedroom in the "upstairs" part of our trailer, and another was located at the rear of the trailer close to a screen window.

The cooler at the rear of the trailer held many gallons of water, so we did not have to fill it as often as the one in our bedroom. The one upstairs held little water, because its tank was much smaller. I should have kept a record of how much water they took on a very hot day. However, no matter how much water it took, it was a very small price to pay for cool air. When you consider that each unit used the equivalent of a 150-watt light bulb, it is amazing how economical evaporative coolers were.

The first part of this verse is always refreshing to read, and it reminds me how grateful we were for the cool fifth wheel trailer home we enjoyed during the warm months of the year: ***they heard the LORD God walking in the garden in the cool of the day.*** (Genesis 3:8)

GATED COMMUNITY

T he trip from mid-Arizona to northwestern Arizona went smoothly. Our drive across the desert was always interesting. I remembered the times I had driven trucks across it from Phoenix to different bases in California getting war surplus material for the Arizona school system. We were glad for air-conditioning in the truck, as the outside temperature was HOT.

Arriving at the host church in Kingman was nice. With proper maps and beforehand preparation, we drove right to the church. A call to the pastor's house brought him to the church quickly, and he showed us the spot to park our fifth wheel trailer. The church parking lot was asphalt, and we backed the unit into a space behind the church where we had a full hook-up. I must admit, I never mastered the art of backing our trailer into place. Sometimes it went well, other times it was difficult. This time, things went pretty well. Margie would guide me into the spot using our cell phones.

Setting up a trailer was routine, but it takes time. Margie did the inside and I did the outside work. Immediately we had our first problem. The pastor had already warned us about bullhead stickers. Some may not know what they are, but they are very nasty pointed seeds of a weed-plant. They are ugly and look something like a bull, and thus their name, bullhead. If you were barefooted, you would be in deep trouble.

Wearing shoes, the stickers cling to them, driving their sharp barbs deep into the leather or rubber of the sole. I noticed different size boards stacked near the wall of the church. I used these and some of our rugs and rubber mats to make a *sidewalk,* so we could enter the trailer without tracking in scores of those annoying stickers. I got the water and sewer connections taken care of and our set up done. It was very rustic, but safe inside the chain-link fence at the rear of the church.

To get a head start on our Sunday ministries, we set up the display table and got some of the projection equipment ready for our Power Point and video presentations. Sunday morning, as usual, we had the Sunday school hour and the morning service. We also had the evening service, and the folks were very receptive. The pastor was extra generous with his pulpit, giving us plenty of time to present the Shepherds ministry.

After our introduction to the church, I gave my usual words about Shepherds, and then said, "Thanks for your wonderful hospitality and the privilege of parking our rig in this very nice gated community." The church erupted into laughter and applause. They loved it, and so did we. ***Distributing to the needs of the saints, given to hospitality.*** (Romans 12:13) They certainly did this.

GETTING A LARGE CHARGE

In Hemet, California, we found our host church and looked for someone who could show us where to park. The church was very nice, with landscaped parking lots and flowerbeds. They had no particular place for us to park our rig, which is always a concern. Finally, they decided we could park at the rear of the building on one of their parking lots, close to the church. It was definitely not a secluded area.

We went through the regular steps of setting up, and this time we made the water hose and electrical extension cord bright with yellow duct tape. We hoped this would alert passers-by to be careful. This was near one of the church exit doors, and so many people would be walking by our trailer.

SOLAR PANES ON CHURCH

The church janitor was helpful as we set up our display. One thing we had noticed as we drove into the parking lot was that the entire back church roof was apparently made of glass. We did not fully understand this until the janitor explained some of the unusual workings of this beautiful big church building. He told us what we saw on the roof were solar panels. The church had opted to install them in order to cut down on their electric bill, which was high, because the building was huge. An unusual thing happened when they switched on the building lights. The place was highly illuminated, and the main electric meter, which would normally turn clockwise, reversed itself and rotated in the opposite direction. We had never heard of such a thing until that moment. You who use solar energy, know better than I how to explain this. Therefore, instead of drawing energy from the local power company, the meter would stop, and then the church's system would feed back into it and use the electricity produced by the solar panels on the roof of the church. This meant the church was not using the local power company's electricity, but their own. What a miracle! We understand the initial cost to install this system was very expensive, but in time it paid for itself by the great savings it provided.

What a wonderful time we had at this church! We met some retired pioneer missionaries and other dear people while there. What a joy to travel and have these added blessings as we went from church to church. After the service, we broke camp in Hemet, and headed back to Stockton, California, our temporary headquarters in that area. In writing thank you letters to these churches that were so good to us, this verse seems appropriate: ***But I hope to see you shortly, and we shall speak face to face. Peace to you. Our friends greet you. Greet the friends by name.*** (3 John 1:14)

GO AHEAD AND DO IT ALL

W e discovered that some pastors did not want us to have the morning service because they wanted to preach. They did not say this, but I was a pastor and loved to expound Scriptures, so I knew where they were coming from.

From our perspective, we earnestly desired to give the church as much information as possible so they could pray more intelligently for the ministry. At one church, the pastor was very happy to have us present Shepherds in Sunday School, which we did gladly, and the folks received it well.

A wonderful thing happened that morning. As I was doing the Sunday School presentation, the pastor was paying very close attention. With the Power Point visual lessons, I gave personal stories which were very interesting for someone new to this ministry. We always wanted to let folks know what Shepherds was doing to care for those with developmental difficulties and the impact made on clients and families.

That morning as I closed the Sunday School hour, the pastor and I went and sat at the front of the auditorium, where he prepared the video machine for the film about Shepherds we would show in the morning service. This was all I would do during the church service. I questioned the pastor how much he wanted me to say to introduce the video. I could tell he liked the Sunday School presentation. He turned to me and said, "Ralph, do it all." He made the decision right there, not to preach, but to allow me to have the entire service. We were thrilled! When you realize that we probably only got to a church every four or five years, or more, we really wanted to give them as much information as possible. We were grateful to the pastor and thanked the Lord for changing his mind. This church was way off the beaten path but was well attended. How we appreciated the pastor's kindness in giving us both morning services! Our travels to churches were something like what Paul and his companions did. We were telling them what God was doing at Shepherds for those with developmental difficulties. *Now when they had come and gathered the church together, they reported all that God had done with them, and that He had opened the door of faith to the Gentiles.* (Acts 14:27)

GOD'S HANDIWORK IN NATURE

F or many years in our ministry in Brazil, Ferndale, and Shepherds, I have used a series of studies I researched about nature. I have always been amazed with the variety in God's creation and the myriads of insects, animals, and plant life He made to inhabit this big world of ours. Recently, a woman from Brazil who attended a church near Natal, Brazil, where we worked, wrote in answer to our blog, saying how as a little girl she remembered my nature stories and the magic tricks I used to present the gospel. I must admit I enjoyed doing this, and I have quite an enormous collection. I continue to add to it, and I use them all the time.

When we were invited to have a Bible study at an adult camp at Warm Springs, Idaho, and later at Camp Pinewood in McCall, Idaho, I decided to use one or two of these amazing facts about nature as I started my Bible lesson each day. I was overwhelmed with the response. In fact, I made a discovery that the attendees to those camps enjoyed the nature studies as much as if not more than the Bible studies. When I ask the classes if they would like a nature study before the Bible study, I always get an enthusiastic, YES!

When you realize that our loving Lord created over 2,000 different species of Praying Mantis alone, or 900 different kinds of crickets, you can see why my extra nature studies were rewarding. In other words, I never cease to be amazed at the vastness of God's handiwork and the enormous intricacy and complexity of His creations. Lord willing, I will do these studies until the Lord takes me home, because I enjoy studying them. Paul makes it clear that God's handiwork is so obvious that no one is without excuse, looking at the work of His hands. ***For since the creation of the world His invisible attributes are clearly seen, being understood by the things that are made, even His eternal power and Godhead, so that they are without excuse.*** (Romans 1:20)

GOING THE EXTRA MILE

W e wrote in another chapter about the church that hosted our visit to Anchorage, Alaska, Dimond Boulevard Baptist Church. They not only provided housing, but also transportation. To us this was an unbelievably kind gesture. We will never forget their gracious deeds for Shepherds and us.

Included in a "package" pastor Andy Frey gave us, was also transportation. He shuffled his family cars to accommodate our travels to distant points. What a wonderful help they extended to us!

In the above-named church there was a couple, the LeMiers, Ted and Donna, who manifested a keen interest in our ministry. They entertained us often and took us sightseeing to several significant landmarks in the Anchorage area. We appreciated so much their hospitality. When our meetings were farther away from Anchorage, Donna LeMier offered us her personal vehicle for these trips. We were overwhelmed. She had a very nice car that served us well on longer trips. We will never forget her unselfishness in providing our transportation. As strangers in an unknown city, the LeMiers' help to us was invaluable. We were and are impressed how God puts a generous spirit in some people's hearts. We thank God for the Anchorage church and the Frey and LeMier families for their help to us with their vehicles. Isaiah may have had something else in mind when he wrote these words, but surely, they apply to us in our experience in Anchorage. ***But a generous man devises generous things, And by generosity he shall stand.*** (Isaiah 32:8)

HELPING THE INTERPRETER

W hile parked in the Los Angeles area, at Calvary Baptist Tabernacle, Gardena, we conducted meetings for Shepherds in other cities as well. The Mexican Baptist pastor invited us to present Shepherds ministry at his church. We did this, using an interpreter. We enjoyed being with the Mexican believers that day. Even though we do not speak Spanish, we had lived in Benjamin Constant, Brazil, for many years. This town was where three nations merged, all having their borders close to us. We spoke Portuguese, and the people in Peru and Colombia spoke Spanish. We understood one another even though we were not fluent in the other language.

At the Spanish church that day, we had a wonderful time. Normally the Latin cultures sing more heartily than we do, and it reminded us so much of our work in Brazil. Many words in each language are similar; only the pronunciation differs. I preached and told them about Shepherds ministry. In the process of preaching and explaining, one has to speak in short sentences, then pause, while the interpreter speaks in his language to the congregation.

At one point in the message, I could tell the interpreter did not know the right word to use. There was a pause, and it was obvious the man just could not bring up the word he needed. Fortunately, at that moment, the thing I was talking about was easy for me, because even in our limited knowl-edge of Spanish, we did know some words. At the precise time when our interpreter could not remember the right word to complete the interpretation, I blurted out the cor-rect word in Spanish. The whole congregation exploded in laughter. As far as the congregation was concerned, I did not know Spanish, and the interpreter was unable to provide the correct translation. When I spoke the correct word, the audience was amazed, and they laughed and laughed. That was a fun moment, and not even the interpreter was embar-rassed. Our words are very important, and we should always be careful to say the right thing. ***Let the words of my mouth and the meditation of my heart Be acceptable in Your sight, O LORD, my strength and my Redeemer.*** (Psalm 19:14)

HOW DID HE REMEMBER THIS?

―――――◆―――――

We were in Arizona visiting churches to present the Shepherds ministry. At many of the churches during a special social time either before or after a service, we met friendly folks who were interested in this ministry.

A woman approached us saying she used to work at Shepherds. She knew our daughter Joy and spoke highly of Shepherds and how much they did to help individuals with developmental disabilities. We questioned her about many things and were deeply interested in her personal acquaintance and work with our daughter. I asked for permission to take a picture of her, which she gladly granted.

Later in our travels, I remembered the conversation with this woman and decided to do something different. We knew Dr. Andrew Wood, the founder and first director of Shepherds, and appreciated his keen memory. I e-mailed him a personal letter and attached a photo of the woman who told us she worked at Shepherds years ago. Then I asked him if he knew who she was.

Soon after this, Dr. Wood responded to my letter and then proceeded to detail much about this woman. He gave her name, work ethic, personality, and told us how long she worked for Shepherds. I printed it off, and it filled an entire page. We were amazed. Repeatedly we were impressed with his ability to recall information. As we traveled for Shepherds, he would read our reports and sometimes write a note about some incident that took place in a given church or town where we were traveling. We rejoiced that in his senior years that ability has been evident many times as we exchanged correspondence. We praise the Lord for this servant who founded Shepherds ministry and faithfully directed it for many years. Dr. Wood's example is obvious in this verse: ***Let no one despise your youth, but be an example to the believers in word, in conduct, in love, in spirit, in faith, in purity.*** (1Timothy 4:12) Although he is not a youth, his example lingers on.

HOW DO WE GET THERE?

———◆———

We were always home for Christmas. We organized our itinerary so we could be with family during that special time. After Christmas, our next scheduled meeting was in El Centro, California. In wintertime in Oregon and California we always faced the challenge of the mountains, especially when we traveled with the fifth wheel.

We had no problems this time going over the Siskiyou Pass, and we wondered what the weather conditions would be as we were getting nearer to Bakersfield. Our normal route was highway 58 from Bakersfield going east, then south to hook up with US 10, which took us to the highway leading to El Centro. The weather report in Bakersfield was not good. There was a road closure on Highway 58 for trucks due to heavy wind and snow conditions. This meant our shortcut was no longer an option.

We next chose Interstate 5 going over the famous Grapevine Pass. We soon discovered that the Highway Department had also closed Grapevine Pass. Now what do we do? We always travelled these routes, so now we did not know where to go. After prayer for wisdom, we considered our options; we only had one more. We headed to the coast and soon were on Highway 101, which follows the coast southward. At least this time we were not plagued with icy, snowy roads. It was longer, but we finally made it to the general area of Los Angeles.

It was five or six PM when we got on Highway 215 heading east. With the millions of people getting off work, you can imagine the condition of the freeways. They were jammed, and many times, we were just creeping along. This went on for hours, and finally the traffic lessened, and we were on our way to El Centro.

It was obviously too late for us to arrive in El Centro that night, so we chose a nice place to park our rig in one of the towns along the highway. Arriving at the trailer park, we saw that there was no vacancy. Now we were in trouble. Where could we spend the night? There were no RV parks anywhere. In desperation, we drove to a Walmart parking lot and found a security guard who kindly showed us where we could park.

It was cold, very late, and we were exhausted. We were thankful for a place to park. We bedded down and made it through the night okay. We had no electricity, because at that point in our travels we did not yet have our nice Honda generator. We were very glad for a good night and a new day. Through it all, God reminded us of a Psalm that we have appreciated many times: *It is vain for you to rise up early, To sit up late, To eat the bread of sorrows; For so He gives His beloved sleep.* (Psalm 127:2)

HOW DO YOU TRANSLATE THAT?

B ecause we lived many years in Brazil, we appreciated anyone involved in translation. We remember vividly how visitors would come to our station, and when we invited them to say a word to our believers, we always had to interpret for them. What usually happened was the person speaking was preoccupied with his message and spoke for a long time without pausing. At some point, he or she would stop and by then the interpreter had *lost them*. An interpreter would have to be very gifted to remember huge sentences involving complicated words, phrases, numbers and many other things.

I have often thought that the way some people speak through an interpreter is confusing. The interpreter probably leaves out a portion of it or just makes up his own story that corresponds to the theme of the message. I do know it is very humbling for the interpreter to do his work when others of his same language group are present. He is under unbelievable pressure, wanting to do his job correctly but all the while knowing his colleagues would probably explain how they would have said such and such if they had been doing the interpreting

Well, that is one side of interpreting, and here is another. When I had to use an interpreter to get a message to a group, I had my own idea how I would do it. Thankfully, most of the times I did this, the language was Spanish. Fortunately for me, we could understand enough to know if the interpreter was really telling the group what we wanted to say. My approach was to speak in very short sentences, stop, let the interpreter translate, and then go on to the next point. While doing it this way, I never had a problem.

The audience had to be patient during these times. For instance, I may say something that my interpreter does not understand. He will stop, ask me to clarify my point to him, and then continue the translation.

We were in Glendale, Arizona, at Faith Baptist Church. It was a bilingual church, English and Spanish. Each language had its pastor. Richard Briningstool and Enoch Arelliano were the pastors. You could tell by their names which church they represented. It was a joy fellowshipping with this church. We appreciated each pastor and his congregations. When Jesus spoke these words, it included those who spoke English and Spanish: ***And He said to them, "Go into all the world and preach the gospel to every creature.*** (Mark 16:15)

HUCKLEBERRY HAVEN

———◆———

Surprises awaited us around every corner, it seemed. We left Lake Blaine Camp ground near Kalispell and were making our way to Heart Butte, Montana. Heart Butte was way out on Indian Reservation country.

As we left Lake Blaine and got on Highway 2 going towards the Great Divide, we kept seeing signs about huckleberries. There were many signs with all sorts of tantalizing pictures and advertising. They invited us to try pies, cakes, ice cream, jelly, jam, candy, and a host of other things, all made from huckleberries. Curiosity got the best of us. We took advantage of the stop to fill the gas tanks by investigating a store that apparently featured huckleberries in about anything you desired to buy. You could purchase pictures of huckleberries growing in the wild, ornately decorating plates, or endless things this store had to honor the huckleberry.

We decided ice cream would be our choice to savor this delicious fruit flavor. We were not disappointed. We were also looking for gifts to give the people who so lovingly cared for our mail and house while were gone representing Shepherds. We finished this delicious ice cream treat as we drove along the highway.

It was obvious that this particular part of the country was indeed a haven for huckleberries. It was more than that. We discovered there is a culture that develops around the growing and harvesting of this favored fruit. We recall that even in our part of Washington State, a man used to take guests with him in search of huckleberries in the appropriate season of the year. Out in Montana we learned more and more about it. People in search of huckleberries would secretly claim a certain spot where there was a bountiful supply. I do not know how one could set claim to a huckleberry bush, but I believe it was serious business for some. Someone would discover a plant in a very inaccessible place on the mountainside. We also wondered if an individual who owned the property could fence off the area so no one could steal the berries. At any rate, we saw that competition was at play in the quest for huckleberries. It appeared to us, in talking to the locals, that it was not a good idea to invade another's territory in huckleberry season. Imagine the Creator of the universe allowing these berry bushes to be prolific in some areas, all for the sheer enjoyment and profit of many who enjoyed picking these berries. God talks a lot about fruit in the Bible, and He wants people to enjoy what the earth yields for our well-being. ***Then the land will yield its fruit, and you will eat your fill, and dwell there in safety.*** (Leviticus 25:19)

HUMOR AT CHURCH

W e were parked at a church in eastern Washington. Our Shepherds meetings were going well, and we even had opportunity to attend other meetings in the church, because we had nothing scheduled during the week for Shepherds. It is always a blessing to interact with fellow-believers in the churches.

Have you ever noticed that sometimes things happen unintentionally that instantly bring a smile? We witnessed such in the church where we were parked. During one of the services, they invited us to speak and show our Shepherds video. The service went well, with good congregational singing, special music, testimonies, and even choir numbers. We really enjoyed our time there.

After the choir sang, they left the choir loft and sat in the auditorium. The audiovisual man was warming up his machines to show our video. As the machine warmed up, it went through a routine, and as the choir members left the loft, their heads were at the same level where the pictures showed on the screen. At one point, the warm-up message flashed exactly above a person's ears and stretched from the front his face to the rear of his head. All it said was "blank". The implication was powerful but extremely ill timed. Who would ever guess that the split second projection would happen in such a fashion? Well, we are sure not many people even saw it, nor did I ever mention it to anyone except my wife. Now I am telling you as I write these lines. In the quietness of the moment and the uniqueness of the circumstances, this was something funny we will never forget. The person who received the sign on his head knew absolutely nothing about it, and I am so glad he did not. In this article we did not intended to demean anyone; we only mention it because the timing and the situation were funny when it happened. We are so glad the Lord allows humor in our lives. The Bible is full of it if we know what to look for. We trust you are a content, happy Christian who can enjoy a good laugh occasionally. Notice what Solomon said. *A time to weep, And a time to laugh; A time to mourn, And a time to dance.* (Ecclesiastes 3:4)

I CAN'T SEE HIS EYES

―――――――◆―――――――

We found the Henderson Avenue Baptist Church in Porterville, California. Behind the church there was place we could park our rig. We met the pastor for the first time, and we were anxious to acquaint this church with the ministry of Shepherds. We attended the Sunday School, and during the morning service talked about Shepherds ministry. The church was very receptive to the message, and after church at the display table Margie and I could answer many questions for them.

My custom at all the churches was to take pictures of the churches and the pastor and his family. The next day, I would send our report to Shepherds concerning Sunday ministries in the various churches, and post a picture of the pastor and his wife and children. I took a picture of this pastor and wife and their two children, a boy and a girl.

Next day when I downloaded the pictures from the camera, I was horrified to note that the family picture was okay except the pastor's glasses reflected the light and you could not see his eyes. Therefore, I had a job to do. I got out my graphic software on the laptop computer and went to work to try to improve this photo. My problem was that the pastor's eyes were literally missing. The sheen on the glasses hid them, making his eyes non-existent. I thought about this for a while and came up with an idea. The pastor's son, I reasoned, had his dad's genes, and so maybe I could clone the son's eyes and give his dad "sight". I carefully cloned the boy's eyes, made copies of the right and left eyes, and then enlarged them slightly – making them the right size for an adult. However, what do I do with the sheen on the glasses? I used the software and took it away so they would appear as clear lenses. Now the photographer must carefully place the cloned eyes under the glass lenses of each eye. Bingo! It happened. Now the father's picture looked as natural as if he were standing there looking at us. What a blessing to have software to help us out in situations like this. I posted the picture, and no one would know it had been edited. All I could do was thank the Lord for helping me do this. It was nothing great on my part. I just had to learn how to use the software correctly. ***In everything give thanks; for this is the will of God in Christ Jesus for you***. (1 Thessalonians 5:18)

I THINK IT IS GOING TO TIP OVER

W e parked our fifth wheel trailer at Tabernacle Baptist Church of Gardena, California. Margie was busy with Pastor Solomon's wife, Susan, in one of the church buildings. They were doing some work for an activity planned for the children or women of the church. I was alone in the trailer making calls to churches, seeking invitations to present the Shepherds ministry. Pastor Solomon was gone, taking a friend to the Los Angeles International Airport.

Using my cell phone and computer, I kept busy making calls to churches.

I took a break and then I started in again. Suddenly, I had a dizzy sensation and realized the trailer was rocking from side to side. It was a strong earthquake. My first thought was the trailer door. If the unit turned on its side toward the door, I could not get out. I did not panic, and soon it was over. I called Margie, but got no answer. In fact, no phones were working. There was a blackout.

Soon afterward, Pastor Solomon returned from the airport on the busy 450 Interstate highway. When I asked him about the earthquake, he realized he did not know anything thing about it. People in cars on the freeway could not feel the shifting. How I thank the Lord for the safety He provided for me in a situation that could have been very dangerous.

The Lord is good, a stronghold in the day of trouble, and he knows those who trust in Him. (Nahum 1:7

IF DUMP STATIONS COULD TALK!

———◆———

When we were missionaries, one of our colleagues had a friend who either invented or owned a motor home that never needed a dump station. In our years on the road or since, we have never encountered such a vehicle. That would be a great invention. Our friend said that somehow the exhaust heat transferred to a special mechanism, which burned the waste material and discharged the safe residue. Wow, what a wonderful deal!

All the years we were on the road, we were concerned about finding the next place where we could empty the holding tanks. One learns some interesting ways to do this. A chain of well-known truck stops had very nice dumping stations, which were a blessing to us. Entering a town, we would get on the computer and search for such a place. Many times, we made numerous phone calls asking where we could find one.

Interstate highways often have them at rest stops. At times, we heard rumors that the state was going to close these. At special holidays sometimes, the lineup for dumping was so long that it would take hours for our turn. In addition, people were thoughtless, and some of these sites were deplorable in the way waste was disposed of. Some would discharge their holding tanks for shower and kitchen water without even putting it properly into the tanks for this purpose. At other times, the carelessness displayed in disposing of the bathroom waste was a disgrace. We just had to learn to take it in stride and put up with it.

We were not guiltless, either. As careful as we tried to be, we made mistakes. In Scottsdale, Arizona, a person told us that a court had such a dumpsite. We spoke with the manager, who invited us to use the facility. Nearby neighbors had warned us not to do it. We could not understand, because the management said it was okay. When I placed the dump hose into the receptacle and opened the valve on the trailer, the thing overflowed immediately and spread sewage all over the back yard of this person's unit. Was that embarrassing? Yes! I spent hours hosing down this mess with fresh water until it was finally clean and presentable again. Had I learned my lesson? I hope so!

We had some very good experiences with dump stations along the way. At one church, we had to drive about twenty-five miles to a dump spot along the ocean at a state facility. We had to check in, pay a fee, and dump. It was always a process, but we were grateful for it. Then we heard of a place that was only blocks away. We were so happy to find this new place, which took much less time every seven days. Yes, we dumped the tanks every seven days. The only way we could get around this time limit is when they allowed us to let out the kitchen sink wastewater onto a lawn or drainage ditch. Those times were rare.

At a church in Arizona, we traveled a very long distance each seventh day to dump at a far-away place. Then in snooping around the church one day, I noticed at the front a cap on a pipe. This was about the size of a dump tube, and I asked the pastor if I could try it and see if it was a connector to the sewage system. It was, and that transformed our stay at that church. Even though we had to take down everything on the trailer, hook it to the truck, and take it just a few hundred feet away, it was worth it. The same thing happened in Stockton, California, when I asked the church officials if I could experiment with another capped pipe near our trailer. Sure enough, it was good, and from then on, we saved the ten-mile trip every seventh day.

The irony of this is that at our home in Ferndale we did not have a hook up. I guess we really did not need one, except it would have been nice when we had guests. However, we gave them our rooms in the house, and we used the trailer. The biggest blessing we received in our travels was when the church had a full hook up. It was so nice not to have to move so much. We experienced wonderful hospitality from all the churches. It is obvious they were fulfilling Paul's command, ***Distributing to the needs of the saints, given to hospitality***. (Romans 12:13)

CHAPEL TIME

Margie and I never wanted to miss Shepherds chapel. Monday through Friday, and Sunday at the same time, residents made their way to the gymnasium for chapel. Some were more mobile, and got there quickly. Our daughter Joy was very slow in making her way to the meeting place. They started her early, but for some reason we will never know, she insisted on being the last one there. In her walker, she clumsily made her way to chapel. Joy was very curious, and as she made her way to chapel, she had to look in each room and through all windows to check on things. Another reason for her being last is she wanted all her roommates to be ahead of her. If any lingered behind, she would stop and wait until they were ahead of her. She did this all her years at Shepherds.

Chapel started when everyone sat down. You would have to be there to enjoy their singing. They all seemed to know the songs, and they loved to sing. Sometimes the leader would have some come up front and form a "choir". Then the director would call on a resident to lead in prayer. I wish you could hear them pray. They were so sincere and honest talking to God.

At offering time, selected individuals passed the plates down the rows of seats. What an experience it was to attend chapel at Shepherds. I spoke at chapel sometimes, and it was a privilege to see the respect, joy and participation of the residents. We learned a lot from these dear ones as they worshipped. ***Oh come, let us worship and bow down; Let us kneel before the LORD our Maker.*** (Psalm 95:6)

CHRISTMAS DRIVE-THROUGH
AT SHEPHERDS

O ur yearly trips to Shepherds at Christmas were always a treat. Besides enjoying our daughter Joy and all the other residents, we were there at a very festive time of the year. For years, the representatives enjoyed a special food and fun night at a nearby restaurant. This was a very fun time.

At the end of each year, toward the end of our stay, Shepherds sponsored a banquet specially to honor all the staff who faithfully ministered at Shepherds. The meal was fabulous and the program a delight. This week was a highlight for us, and all the staff. For the staff to attend this gala event, previous arrangements had to be made. A church in Milwaukee, Spring Creek, had many who volunteered to travel twenty-five miles to Shepherds to assume the responsibility of caring for residents that evening.

One year we encountered in this group some very dear friends, former missionaries with ABWE, in Brazil, Art & Joyce Cavey. What a great time we enjoyed, visiting with them and recounting some stories of years ago when we knew them in Brazil.

An impressive event took place each year at Shepherds that was so very special. They had a Christmas drive-through, at which time the Shepherds residents acted out the Christmas story. They did a wonderful job telling the story of Jesus. They distributed Gospel literature so that all who visited would have something tangible to take home. Simultaneously with the drive through, special events were taking place in the large recreational center. What a blessing for us to see and hear, as separate groups from Shepherds mounted the risers to give a Christmas musical rendition. What a blessing as the angel announced to the shepherds that night long ago, ***"Do not be afraid, for behold, I bring you good tidings of great joy which will be to all people. (Luke 2:10)*** Each year the Shepherds residents gave to Union Grove, Wisconsin, these good tidings.

CLIENTS MINISTERING TO OTHERS

Even though we had a mentally challenged daughter, we never really knew how much these dear children and adults ministered to us and others. As far as our daughter is concerned, we are convinced she ministered to people even though she never spoke a word in her fifty-two years. Her life touched many as we had opportunity to share her story, but she taught us as her parents, the most.

Individuals with disabilities are greatly misunderstood and underestimated. One day a Shepherds resident met a family whose son had died. He immediately ministered to this grieving family by singing them a hymn of comfort. In my experience, I probably would not have sung a song to grieving parents, but on the other hand, this fine young man may have had a better way to minister than I did. We were impressed to hear how he touched many lives in such a positive way.

On another occasion, a client was visiting in an area that had recently been devastated by tornadoes. The church was unusable for holding a meeting, so they rented another building for their services. Mr. Al Pick reported how this godly young man spoke to the congregation, telling them that God would supply what they needed, and in God's time they would be back in their church facility worshipping the Lord. What a gracious way to minister to a hurting church family!

One of the Shepherds men traveled to churches to sing ***It will be worth it all when we see Jesus,*** *and give his tes-timony.* His singing has blessed countless thousands. Only eternity will reveal how many people this song has helped. Sometimes the words are slow in coming, but he always managed to sing the powerful song, which has blessed so many. One time when he made a long pause in his singing, another resident approached him and said, "It is okay, Jesus will help you". About that time, the words came to him, and he finished the song. Dr. Andrew Wood, former President of Shepherds, told us this story. Someone who was there said that many in the audience shed tears.

Someday we will understand just how much these dear friends have ministered to others. This powerful word from Paul reminds me how we should use our voices for God's glory. ***Let the word of Christ dwell in you richly in all wisdom, teaching and admonishing one another in psalms and hymns and spiritual songs, singing with grace in your hearts to the Lord.*** (Colossians 3:16)

COINCIDENCE

---❖---

In our travels for Shepherds, we thought we had seen and experienced just about every type of situation, but in Polson, Montana, we were surprised by what we experienced.

At First Baptist Church in Polson, pastor Rudy Ringhoff invited the Maranatha College musical team for a presentation in their church. The church filled with folks who came to hear this group perform. As the team sang different numbers, they interspersed their personal testimonies, giving us an idea of who each one was and a little bit about them.

Soon, we observed an interesting pattern developing as each person spoke and sang. Our first surprise was the word given by the pianist of the group, Sarah Delaney. In her introduction, she mentioned she grew up in Singapore. That was very interesting! My brother and his wife have been missionaries in Singapore for over 63 years. Even though Singapore is a small island country, this girl did not know my brother. What a coincidence!

The next young man who spoke was Jeremiah Wilson from Crato, Brazil. Could it be we knew his father and grandfather when we lived and worked in Brazil? Yes, we did. We had a delightful time speaking the Portuguese language as we visited with him. What a coincidence!

To our surprise, the next one who spoke was Jean Sturtz, from Ferndale, Washington. This is the small town where we

318

live. We did not know her, but she was from our hometown. What a coincidence!

Others from that musical group had equally interesting situations that made our evening very special. I have often said how wonderful the Lord was to program many people into our lives as we traveled about. What a blessing to fellowship with believers in different situations and locations! I am sure this idea comes from these words from Scripture: ***And they continued steadfastly in the apostles' doctrine and fellowship, in the breaking of bread, and in prayers.*** (Acts 2:42)

COMMUNICATION CHALLENGES

———————◆———————

L et us face it: most of us are *hooked* on cell phones. To do our Shepherd's ministry effectively, we had to communicate with not only churches, but also the home base in Union Grove, Wisconsin

At first, it was all so new to us that we did what we could with what we had. Parked at Lake Blaine, Near Kalispell, Montana, we had the problem of how to keep in touch with churches, family, and Shepherds. I asked permission from the camp director to use the phone line in the camp kitchen, and he said it was okay. I tapped into it because I carried a lot of telephone wire for such a need as this. I carried a couple of phones and used one in our trailer. When the phone rang, I answered it, because we were the only ones at camp. I could help any who called with a specific question by giving them the name of the person responsible they should call. I also used this line to make calls for Shepherds. When it became obvious that the camp paid for long distance calls, I went to the local phone company in Kalispell, Montana, where we made special arrangements so I could pay for my calls. It worked out very well. During camps it was better we not use this special line to our trailer.

That was not the end of our telephone line use. In Stockton, California, we used the phone in the nearby Sunday School building, next to our trailer. I had a miniature telephone that fit in the palm of my hand with a headset and microphone. I could dial and make calls very nicely. I would only use that line when the pastor was not in his office, and this worked well.

At one of our stops along the way, I visited a Verizon Wireless shop and inquired about getting our laptop hooked to the outside world. I purchased an air card and learned how to do things one normally does with a computer. With the air card, we could do business just as we did when at home.

Parked outside a church in Fortuna, we had the blessing of tapping into the code of the church Wi-Fi. We were able to use our computer in the trailer without even having to go inside the church. The signal was strong enough in our trailer for that. How good can it get! In that same city, we visited the headquarters of C. Crane Radio and purchased a cell phone antenna. It was very good. It had a short antenna with a magnetic base. From it, we had a long wire inside the trailer hooked directly to the cell phone. We normally had a cell phone that did not receive a signal, but with this simple set up, ours would. It was very useful for us in places where signals were weak. I remember we were in the Blackfoot Indian Reservation in Heart Butte, Montana. The pastor of the church where we parked our trailer told us that at his house there was no cell phone communication at all. At the church, he said it was very poor. We parked there for many days, and thanks to good connections, we had contact with the world, and we were very thankful.

At camp Lake Blaine, they told us about a magic circle just outside the chapel front door where one could stand to get a signal. Our parking place was quite a distance from that magic circle, but because of the special antenna, we received perfect signals. All this was because we had that dandy antenna. The years we spent on the road, communication was indeed a blessing from the Lord. We rejoiced that we could keep up with the world via our laptop and cell phone. I will mention our other miracle in another story. Each time we secured an appointment to have a meeting, these words of Paul were our prayer as we thanked them for inviting us: *that I may come to you with joy by the will of God, and may be refreshed together with you.* (Romans 15:32)

CULTURE OF A LAUNDROMAT

W hen at the Baptist church in Castaic, California, we had a nice place to park our rig. The church folks were very kind to us, and we appreciated them very much. They always welcomed us, and we ministered there more than once.

On the road, a weekly chore was getting our clothes washed. Our fifth wheel trailer did not have a washing machine, so we used our computer to search out laundromats in the area. In Castaic we found a nice laundromat and frequented it a couple times while in the area. We found that some laundromats were exceptionally well kept, and others dirty and a disgrace. However, in Castaic, God had something special planned for us. As was our custom, we tried to befriend people in order to talk to them about our ministry and witness to them. I noticed a man who seemed to be down in his spirit, so I cautiously began talking to him. The more I talked to him the more I realized he was hurting but was not telling me the whole story.

As we progressed in our conversation, I told him I would be praying for him. I discovered he was a professing Christian, separated from his wife, probably because of some of his own foolish choices. He finally admitted that he should be with his wife. That night, in the laundromat, we had a prayer meeting, and I asked God to give him the strength to admit his wrongs and return to his wife. It was indeed a blessing to have him agree to make contact with his wife and plan a way to reestablish their relationship. That very night he told me he was going to call her.

These are stories we love to tell. We were never able to get the end of this story, but what a joy it was to commit him and his situation to the Lord. We are confident this story ended by a renewed relationship. Margie had a marvelous ministry of leaving Christian literature at laundromats. People do a lot of reading at these places while waiting for their clothes to wash and dry. She carefully selected good Christian material she had read and felt appropriate to leave in these places.

Only eternity will tell how many people have listened to us, taken tracts, etc., and made any kind of a spiritual decision. We pray they have. We discovered long ago that we should not waste opportunities like this. One never knows who may need an encouraging word, especially from God's Word. Peter admonishes us in this verse to keep up the good work: *If anyone speaks, let him speak as the oracles of God. If anyone ministers, let him do it as with the ability which God supplies, that in all things God may be glorified through Jesus Christ, to whom belong the glory and the dominion forever and ever. Amen.* (1 Peter 4:11)

DEER ME

T ravel in Montana for us was a ministry and an adventure. Fortunately, we were not there in the dead of winter, so we did not have the rigors of maneuvering on snow-clad roads and highways. We were thankful for that, but other things demanded our attention.

Before leaving for the church in which we presented Shepherds, the locals had already pre-warned us about the hazards on the roads. We normally traveled early in the morning to our destinations, and these were the critical times for deer to be crossing the highway. How does one drive to a distant point and be prepared for these beautiful animals that dart across the highways, unaware of cars? Well, it was hard, and there was no way we could prepare except to be an alert driver, and pray.

I remember the first time we had an *encounter.* We were in our Ford 250 going about the normal speed limit along the highway. Suddenly a mother deer and two very small babies were in the middle of the road. The babies did not know what to do. It happened so quickly, but thankfully, mother and her family made it to the other side safely. We were ALWAYS on the alert, knowing that at any moment, we could experience this again, and we did many times.

A friend suggested I install some special deer alert whistles on the truck. They are supposed to emit a sound that apparently scares the deer away. I never really knew if they worked or not, but do know that we never hit an animal.

When we parked at Lake Blaine, near Kalispell, Montana, we often attended prayer meeting at the Baptist church in Bigfork, Montana. It was several miles to church, and part of the trip was through farmland. Many times, at night, we met several deer along the way. I remember one night there was an endless chain of incidents. At one place, we turned the corner and eight big deer were looking straight at us. We were going slowly, which was a help. Sometimes we would stop on a rural highway, traffic permitting, and let the deer cross to the other side. Do deer have personalities? I think they do. One time a large deer stopped in the middle of the road and looked at us as if to say, "What are you doing here?" The Bible talks about all the animals God created in this special verse: *For every beast of the forest is Mine, And the cattle on a thousand hills.* (Psalm 50:10)

DEVOTIONS WITH A DELIGHTFUL TOUCH

O ne evening during our yearly visit to Shepherds, a counselor from the men's unit invited us to attend devotions. We were in for a treat, because we had never done this before. The men from several rooms gathered. Margie and I sat down with the men around us as we faced the leader. He was a Shepherds resident, and each time we passed his room, he was reading. Later we heard he also read certain magazines about construction and architecture, because he was intrigued with this subject.

When all the men had arrived, he started by giving a word of exhortation, followed by Scripture reading. He made remarks about the text like a pastor, and then he picked up Our Daily Bread and read an appropriate selection. He made comments about this also.

We observed the men as the leader was speaking. They were listening to him intently. Margie and I were getting another close-up picture of this fabulous group of people, misunderstood by many. Who would think a mentally challenged person could select a portion of Scripture, and after reading it, give some special devotional thought. Well, we learned that night, it happens at Shepherds.

After reading the Daily Bread, the leader announced that it was prayer time. He said we would go around the room and each one would pray. We wish you could have heard them pray, simply, honestly, and fervently. We learned much that evening. Thank God for their training at Shepherds! I thought of the Apostle Paul and his words to Timothy when I saw that fine young man lead devotions. ***Till I come, give attendance to reading, to exhortation, to doctrine.*** (1 Timothy 4:13)

DO NOT THROW IT AWAY

One of our many wonderful experiences while representing Shepherds took place while we were parked at Tabernacle Baptist Church in Gardena, California. The church allowed us to park on the large lot behind the church, where the Toyota Corporation parked their new cars.

We had purchased a television at Walmart in Oregon. In California, it gave out, so we thought the only thing we could do was throw it away. One afternoon, Stan Johnson visited us in our fifth wheel, and for some reason we mentioned the television problem. Stan immediately remarked that we should not throw it away. He had much experience in electronics and for some reason wanted to look at it before we threw it away.

STAN JOHNSON FIXING TV

In a couple of days, he returned with tools and some extra parts and did testing on the television. He was particularly suspicious of a small part in the unit and removed it. As soon as he did, he noticed some white powder around it, which alerted him to the fact that it was probably defective. There are so many parts on a television; I am amazed anyone can figure them out. Further testing of this part indicated it was no good. To our surprise, Stan had several of these capacitors in his kit. He exchanged it and assembled the machine. He turned it on, and it worked perfectly.

We thought a lot about this incident. Stan was from the old school of thought that fixed things instead of throwing them away. To think that such a small piece, about half the length of your index finger, was the solution to the problem! We had personally never had an appliance fixed this way. I guess the usual way to deal with the problem was to throw them away and get a new one. Stan would not charge us for the repair, so we got even with him by buying him a gift certificate at a favorite breakfast diner he often frequented.

The television lasted until we sold our trailer to a fellow-missionary couple when we terminated our ministry with Shepherds. In the Old Testament, when all the articles of the Tabernacle were made, we read, ***Moreover, there are workers with you in abundance: woodsmen and stonecutters, and all types of skillful men for every kind of work.*** King David found men capable of doing the work he needed. How wonderful that still today God equips men and women with gifts to do all sorts of things! I trust you are using your gift for His glory.

DON'T BLOW A FUSE

T hings can get difficult at times. Setting up the fifth wheel trailer was a routine we had to learn. Many churches did not have an outside electrical plug. We have used about every imaginable combination of extension cords and adapter plugs to make necessary connections. I bought many extension cords for the trailer. You cannot buy them at the Dollar Store, because they are commercial and about as thick as your thumb.

Pastors used to ask me, "Do you have an extension cord that will reach that plug?" My answer was this: "I have enough cord to reach from here to there, no matter where *there* is!" In one situation, I used five cords. We put cords through windows door transoms, across lawns, around corners, up into windows on the second floor, and in a few more places.

We discovered, and pastors told us, that churches normally are not set up for these kinds of connections. The amperage in many outlets was insufficient to take the load required by our trailer. As a result, we had plenty of confusing nights at many places. At one place in eastern Washington, the pastor showed us where we could connect our extension cord. It was across a large yard, then across the sidewalk and plugged into the outlet at the side of the church. Then our fun began. In about 15 minutes or less, the lights went out. The pastor had given me a key to the building, but not the exact location of the fuse box. Opening a lot of doors, I finally found the fuse box and tried to find the fuse that had tripped. Locating it, I reset it and returned to the trailer. All this time Margie was waiting in the dark. The fun had only begun. About every half-hour, the fuse would trip and I would return to the room and reset it. Finally, we gave up and just decided to go dark for the night.

GETTING ELECTRICITY TO THE TRAILER

In California one time, parked at a lovely spot by a church, we plugged into the outside set-up, which had its own box. We thought that was good. It tripped after a while, and I had to go out and reset it. I remember as if it were yesterday: as I focused the light on the lever that would reset the fuse, I saw silhouetted in the light a big fat black widow spider, very close to my face. It was awaiting its next meal, but I am glad I saw it first.

One time our lights went out at a church in Montana. This church had a good place to park, and they even had a built-in dump station. The electrical plug was right there by the trailer and supposedly worked well, but that night everything went black. The pastor did not live nearby, and I had no key to the church. I called him, and he told me about a plug near the front door to the church. Sure enough, it was there, but when I extended several large extension cords, it was too short. I would have to get more cord. I glanced at my watch and saw that the Wal-Mart nearby was going to close within fifteen minutes, and I still had to drive there. I arrived at the store, quickly found the cord, and departed just as they closed the door. What a blessing that was!

Sometimes we parked by churches and the power cord had to cross the sidewalk leading into the church. I was extremely careful when this happened and had special bright yellow duct tape which alerted pedestrians to the cord. It was a safety issue, and pastors always appreciated how much concern we had for people's safety. Traveling this way was a learning process, and we were always in need of wisdom from the Lord to know how to handle each situation we faced. ***For the LORD gives wisdom; From His mouth come knowledge and understanding.*** (Proverbs 2:6)

DON'T GET CAUGHT IN THE DARK

---◆---

While traveling to many churches in the Pacific Northwest and other states, we sometimes encountered situations that were challenging. We had to carry with us a variety of adapters. Some were for heavy-duty outlets. Others required only an extension cord through a church window into a classroom. But even these at times required special adapters for the heavy extension cords necessary to run the RV system.

Sometimes, if we did not make it to our desired destination, we would find a service station and ask permission to park in their facility. When doing this, we had no electrical outlet to use. In times like these, we wished we had a generator. We prayed much about this and committed it to the Lord. If He wanted us to have one, He would work it out.

One Sunday at our home church in Ferndale, a couple, Chuck and Cindy Heath, handed me a sizable check that overwhelmed me. About that same week, our son and his wife also gave us a very generous check. With these gifts, we knew we could purchase a small generator. I went online, where I found a very good deal, and ordered it. Did you guess right? Yes, the checks we were given covered exactly the price of a new Honda generator.

HONDA GENERATOR

We were thrilled to have this machine. Sometimes out in the middle of "nowhere" we would start it up and enjoy a good meal and cozy night in our fifth wheel trailer. Certain precautions were necessary in owning such a wonderful machine. Because a Honda generator is so popular and valuable, I went into a hardware store in Clovis, CA and purchased a heavy-duty chain and large padlock. At night when we used the generator, I would put it near the leveling jacks, below the bedroom part of the fifth wheel, and chain and lock it. That way a nosey thief would not be able to "borrow it". While purchasing this chain, the hardware salesperson told me of another man who had come in to buy a chain for his generator, and while he was in the store buying one, thieves stole the generator off his pick-up truck in the parking lot.

You may wonder about the exhaust fumes and the noise of a generator so near the trailer. The amazing thing about the Honda generator is its quietness. It was wonderful! It scarcely made more noise than a few people talking in a room. Fumes never bothered us, even though Margie is highly sensitive to them. We thanked God for the dear friends who made this machine possible for us. We always gave thanks to Him for His goodness in providing our needs. In addition, I should say also, that the little gasoline tank on the machine held enough gas to run for hours without refilling; it was very economical. We thanked the Lord many times for the dear ones God used to supply our need just as the Lord has promised. **And my God shall supply all your need according to His riches in glory by Christ Jesus.** (Philippians 4:19)

DON'T PARK ON THE STREET

———————◆———————

We drove from Fremont, California, to San Francisco for a Shepherd's presentation in the Hamilton Square Baptist Church. We had been there before, so this time we knew our route better. However, driving in San Francisco has its challenges, as you can imagine. Arriving in the more complicated part of the city, we encountered some detour warnings. A parade for a group of people with a different life-style than ours had several blocks closed for the occasion. We finally made it around these detours, with the help of a GPS unit our son gave us. It is a real blessing in our ministry.

Arriving early for the service, we soon found the church entrance, but parking was our main concern. Finally, the custodian approached us and we identified ourselves. He instructed us to come to a certain gate, and he would open it. We followed his instructions and discovered the entryway was just a bit wider than the width of our truck. It took us a while, but we made it, grateful that our truck was in a secure place. He told us that under no circumstances would we want to leave our car on the street. In other words, if the car remained on the street, people would pilfer it. We were very happy we had a good place to park!

The services went well, and all were enthusiastic about the Shepherds ministries. They had supported this work for years. Pastor David Innes and his wife, a delightful couple, entertained us at their home for lunch. At the church, we had opportunity to rest in the guest room, and it was very comfortable. That evening we showed a video and spoke about Shepherds again. The folks were very receptive, and we appreciated their interest in the ministry. We were very impressed with the good attendance in this downtown church where parking is such a concern. We learned that day how the church rents parking garages near the church and issues passes to those desiring to attend. It was a fantastic way to handle the parking problem.

We laud Pastor Innes and this fine church for the wonderful hospitality they gave us; also, the faithful support to Shepherds. That night as we travelled home to Fremont, we gave thanks to the Lord for the privilege of ministering in this fine church. We had only been there twice, but the memory of them is special. Paul said it best: ***For your fellowship in the gospel from the first day until now,*** (Philippians 1:5)

DON'T TAKE THINGS FOR GRANTED

A ppreciation for things done should be the hallmark of our lives. It is so easy to be on the receiving end and forget that it would be good to give also. Margie and I always felt this way in the eight western states where we parked our trailer as we represented Shepherds.

In Stockton, California, at Faith Baptist Church, Pastor and Mrs. David Einer were abundantly kind to us. The place to park was superb, covered with massive shade trees that were more than welcome in the extreme summer heat. Pastor and Mrs. Einer and their church family became very special to us. We noticed that the elaborately made sign on the main street in front of the church was in need of refurbishing. With special power tools, I was able to clean up the background board. Then I varnished it and repainted the black letters spelling out the name of the church and times of services. It was a large sign, and both sides were in disrepair. That project took many hours, but what a joy to make it attractive again. I have painted signs most of my life, so this was "up my alley," as they say.

FAITH BAPTIST CHURCH, STOCKTON

Another part of the church facility that needed attention was the flowerbeds. Margie assumed this task and worked over all of them. There were several, and they were big. It took weeks to get these jobs completed. However, there was more. I noticed that the front door of the church had watermarks caused by the poorly adjusted lawn sprinklers. Several underground watering sprinklers needed repairs or were non-functioning; I took it as a project to fix them. That accomplished, I turned to refinishing the church's front door. I wanted to do this right, so I applied multiple coats of varnish, which took a long time. We were able to squeeze these tasks in between our scheduled Shepherds meetings. It was very important to us to have a safe place to park.

Margie and I earnestly wanted to give these gifts to the church in appreciation for their generous hospitality. Later the church convened while we were absent and took an offering for us. The dear believers in this church blessed us with a card with personal notes and a monetary gift. I guess we just could never get ahead of them. However, we did not take them for granted. What precious memories we have of this wonderful group of believers! They were so good to us and appreciated the ministry of Shepherds. Our hearts fill with thanks each time we think of them, just like Paul for the Philippians. ***I thank my God upon every remembrance of you.*** (Philippians 1:3)

DON'T TOUCH THAT THERMOSTAT!

FIRST BAPTIST CHURCH, WALTERIA, CA

I only wish someone had been able to tell our dear pastor friend this the day it happened. On this Sunday morning, Pastor Currier went across the road to his church and prepared the facility for the morning service. He did the usual things, checking this and that to see if all was ready for the day's activities.

It was winter, so he stepped to the thermostat to turn up the heat. That was the starting point of a very serious explosion. It blew him many feet to one side of the church, where the wall collapsed. He was severely burned, and they took him to emergency.

That is the quick version of the story. Investigators later determined a gas pipeline from the side street that provided gas for the furnace and baptistery water heater was leaking fumes. Just above the baptistery floor, this deadly gas was accumulating in a pocket. When he adjusted the thermostat, a small spark, caused by its two contact points, is what ignited this unbelievable explosion.

Fire detectives reported that the force of the blast was so intense, that it raised the entire roof of the church about four inches from its moorings before it settled back down on the walls. In other areas of the church, the story was tragic. The explosion closed the church for a long time during construction and repairs.

What happened to Pastor Robert Currier? His story is one of God's abundant grace and healing. His visage was practically unrecognizable, and in the burn ward, all marveled that he was still alive. The Christian community rallied in fervent prayer for this dear man of God. His testimony was vibrant through it all. Many visitors came to his room when he was finally able to have company. His pain-racked body never robbed him of his sweet attitude and pleasant personality. His dear wife was with him through the long recovery, giving tender loving care.

Pastor's opportunities for evangelism through this episode were noteworthy. He never lost a moment to praise the Lord for bringing him through this most amazing tragedy. When Margie and I viewed the pictures taken of him in the burn unit, we could hardly believe anyone so badly burned could have survived.

Pastor Currier loved Shepherds and its ministries. We were always welcome in his church to present the ministry. We were there after the church was repaired due to money their insurance policy provided. Thank God for insurance. Pastor was so tender in his remarks about Shepherds, and he always called us even years after we ministered in his church.

Every time we read this verse, we think of Pastor Currier. We have never seen anyone burned so badly, yet show no signs of the disaster. ***When you pass through the waters, I will be with you; And through the rivers, they shall not overflow you. When you walk through the fire, you shall not be burned, Nor shall the flame scorch you.*** (Isaiah 43:2) Since writing this story, Pastor Currier is now present with the Lord. His story is inspirational. His dear wife Hazel June continues to be a blessing to friends and family.

DUST AT THE END OF SUMMER

---◆---

Those of us who do not live in Alaska are not accustomed to the vocabulary used by the locals. This was our experience as we approached the end of our commitment in Anchorage. We enjoyed wonderful times in the State we had never visited before. My brother lived there, but his busy traveling schedule for work prevented us from seeing him much. We knew we would not be able to use their house as our motel while away because all the rooms were filled with family and extra family members for whom they were responsible.

We were always intrigued with the information learned from locals. In August, we had already seen some snowfalls in Anchorage; this apparently is normal. As summer was ending, we kept hearing talk about **termination dust.** Because I was curious, I asked what this phrase meant. They assured me we would soon find out, if we stayed in Anchorage many more weeks.

Sure enough, one morning we looked at the beautiful mountains surrounding Anchorage and noticed it had snowed during the night. However, you could still see the rocks and bushes on the mountainside. It looked like someone had sprinkled white powder on the hillside during the night. We know who that was, the Lord. We watched this phenomenon day after day and the slow accumulation of snow on the mountaintop. As more **dustings** took place, the snow level dropped. All this was a sign to Alaskans that winter was on its way.

The day we left Anchorage to fly to Washington State, I took a picture of the **termination dust** that had inched its way down the mountain, and now it was filling in the darker areas with snow that kept them covered all winter. What a sight it was!

I will mention one more indicator of winter. The fireweed plant is a fascinating study and one which shows again God's great handiwork in nature. This beautiful red flower grows on a stalk, and the progress of blooms accurately predicts winter's arrival. Several phrases describe this flower. One says **the fireweed bloom casts the date for winter.** Another author wrote about it with the title, **winter's clock.** This plant grows up to 8 feet and is an amazing indicator of the seasons. The bloom grows a few inches from the top of the plant when it is about a foot or two high. During the summer months, the petals grow higher. When they reach the tip, summer is apparently over. When the blooms reach the top, the plant turns cottony with seed. Therefore, the locals know that the wind will blow the cotton-laden seeds around for next year's crop, and winter snowflakes are near. What a miracle in nature to help them know the seasons! Solomon told us this: **For everything, there is a season, a time for every purpose under heaven.** (Ecclesiastes 3:1) In addition, when He purposes the winter to begin, He gives several indicators.

EAVES-DROPPING AT THE RESTAURANT

———◆———

We parked our trailer at a church in Stockton, California. This made it easier for us to commute to churches further west near the coast. We preferred making round trips from Stockton to the churches on the coast.

On this particular Sunday, we were in a church near San Leandro. We were blessed by the great reception the people gave us as we talked about Shepherds. At the literature table, they took several pieces that would better acquaint them with the ministry. After the service, the pastor and his wife and daughter took us to a nearby restaurant for a very nice meal and great fellowship. This pastor's daughter was developmentally disabled, and we enjoyed so much her presence with us at the meal. She was intelligent in her own way, and it was a pleasure visiting with her. We knew her parents held a soft spot in their hearts for Shepherds, wondering if someday the door would open for their daughter to be there. What happened after the meal is an unusual story.

We thanked the pastor and his wife and daughter for the good evening service at church and the delicious meal at the restaurant, and then headed for the door. Our truck was parked in the shadows out behind the restaurant parking lot. As we approached the truck, a man stepped from the shadows and began talking to us. I wondered what was going on. His coming from the darkness and talking to a stranger was a little out of the ordinary. He immediately told me that he and his wife were listening to us visit during the meal inside the restaurant. Because he had obviously eavesdropped much of the conversation, he was curious what organization we represented. I told him, and he proceeded to tell me he had been a pastor for years and was presently in the real estate business. He asked if we had any literature about Shepherds. I assured him we did and told him I would be glad to get some as he spoke. I went to the truck and retrieved some from the special storage compartment at the rear of our truck.

Finally, I was at ease that this individual was not a robber wanting money. I confess I thought that at first, because he approached me in the dark. He took the literature, reached for his billfold, took some significant denomination bills of money, and handed them to me. I was rather stunned at what was happening. I asked him for his name and address, which he gave me. We wanted his address so Shepherds could send him a receipt for his very generous gift to the ministry. We exchanged email addresses and parted ways.

All I can say is that we never know how the Lord works in lives. Imagine: a man whom I did not see in the restaurant was listening to our conversation and did this very noble deed in contributing to the ministry. ***And whatever you do, do it heartily, as to the Lord and not to men. (Colossians 3:23)*** There was no doubt about it. This man sincerely wanted to give a contribution to the Lord's work. What a great lesson this was for us. We never know who is listening or watching what we say and do.

FACEBOOK

At a church in central California, we presented the Shepherds ministry. The church allowed us to park our rig in a little-used uphill driveway directly alongside the church. It was our privilege to spend a good many hours with the believers and pastor of this church. It was always a blessing to be able to spend more than just one service in a church. Having this nice parking space allowed us to visit other churches without the inconvenience of moving our rig each time.

Later, the church invited us to return. We were thrilled with the reception given Shepherds both times. The folks showed a genuine interest in the Shepherds ministry. At the conclusion of the service, we were outside near the church entrance visiting with several, including the pastor and his wife. We were overwhelmed with all the questions they asked concerning our ministry and specifically how God was working in our lives. They wanted to know our secret of 57 years of service for the Lord. It was a real privilege to share with them. We were encouraged.

When we returned home after this series of meetings in California, Margie received an email from the pastor's wife of the church described above. She was wondering if Margie had a Facebook page, because she was interested in corresponding with her. Margie and I have often wondered why email was not sufficient. It is very personal, and the entire world cannot tap into your conversation. Yes, we know all about the controls we can set up on these pages, but for us email is easier.

OUR HOME IN FERNDALE

We are not bad-mouthing Facebook. In fact, I just added my photo on with Margie's so we both can use it. One of the great positives of Facebook is this: our Brazilian friends are finding us, and we have made some remarkable discoveries via Facebook. We have been blessed when former seminary students in Natal, Brazil, contact us and renew our friendship. As I write this, one of our friends requested our website and blog addresses. When I sent them, he immediately notified me he would be logging on to them. The Apostle Paul spoke warmly of his desire to see people to whom he was writing: (1Thessaloinians 2:17) *But we, brethren, having been taken away from you for a short time in presence, not in heart, endeavored more eagerly to see your face with great desire.* On Facebook, we usually receive a picture of the ones we have not seen for many years. What a blessing! Seeing these pictures brings back many happy memories. In addition, our picture is there for them to remember to pray for us and we for them.

FIFTIETH ANNIVERSARY SURPRISE

O n August 20, 2004, we celebrated fifty years of marriage. In retrospect, it is hard to believe how fast these years passed. We went to church that morning and attended Sunday School as usual. Then we went into the church auditorium for the worship service. I was in the church foyer, and a woman mentioned to me that I should greet some folks who were entering the church. I glanced at those coming up the stairs, and was shocked to see Mr. Al Pick, my "boss". He is the director of Church Relations for Shepherds Ministries and had come to Ferndale for our anniversary.

ALAN PICK

On this day, because we were home from our travels for Shepherds, we were scheduled to give the presentation in our home church. To have Al Pick there was a privilege we will never forget. At 2 PM that afternoon, the church had a special celebration for our anniversary. Among the various highlights that day was a special video from my brother Ernie, his wife Verda, and their goddaughter, Siang. Ernie gave a challenge from the Word about Aquila and Priscilla, which meant so much to us. Al Pick represented Shepherds, and spoke. We were touched that the administration would send him all the way from Union Grove, Wisconsin, to Washington for our special occasion. During the service, friend Glenn Golay and our son Rawlie sang our wedding song, *Day by Day*; it was beautiful!

Our daughter-in-law, Gina, and her neighbors provided the decorations and refreshments; they did a beautiful job. We were impressed and surprised as so many friends helped us enjoy this special day. There are many surprises as we walk with the Lord. What a wonderful thing to realize that fellowship with Him is such a great opportunity and privilege. We never know what a day will bring forth, but we do know that as we walk with Him, life is never dull. That's what makes every day exciting for the child of God. Only in Christ can one experience such profound contentment. Look at this verse and rejoice with us: *This is the day the LORD has made; We will rejoice and be glad in it.* (Psalm 118:24)

FIRST SUNDAY IN MONTANA

—————◆—————

It was exciting to present the ministry of Shepherds in places we had never been. Most of our initial meetings were new churches to us. We spent many weeks lining up meetings in Montana, and now we were heading for this state known as Big Sky Country. Once you are there, you see that the name is very fitting.

Arriving at First Baptist Church in Polson, Montana, we met Pastor Ringhoff, who showed us the spot to park our trailer. It was very nice, with a full hook up. We seldom enjoyed that treat. We set up our display on Saturday so we would be ready Sunday.

On Sunday morning, they invited us to speak during Sunday School to several of the combined classes and show the Power Point. This church was a friend of Shepherds and supported the ministry long before we visited their church. I preached and presented the work of Shepherds during the worship service. The folks warmly received the message, and it was a blessing to be there and to fellowship with them. When the service was over, we made our way to the display table located in the church foyer. What we saw next was a surprise.

During the services that morning, things were brewing outside. When we approached the display table and looked out the large windows, we saw that the cars and ground were covered with snow. It was the first Sunday in May, and we could hardly believe our eyes. The folks quickly explained, "This is Montana"! They told us these weather patterns were common in Montana and we would doubtless see more of it in the days to come.

We had lunch that day in the home of a lovely couple whose home looked out over beautiful Flathead Lake. This lake is BIG. It is the largest body of water west of the Mississippi River. What a gorgeous view as we ate lunch! This lake stretches from Polson to Kalispell, Montana. Imagine all the lake property; it is quite a sight!

This first meeting in Polson started a long relationship with this state and all the wonderful churches and people. We understand how Paul wrote to the Philippian believers these words: ***For God is my witness, how greatly I long for you all with the affection of Jesus Christ.*** (Philippians 1:8) What a blessing people were to us as we traveled from church to church.

HEARING PORTUGUESE
WHILE SHOPPING

———◆———

Dollar stores come in a variety of sizes, colors, personalities, and a few other things. It was intriguing to see the different kinds of companies as we traveled for Shepherds. For instance, some were so disorderly that they looked more like a dumpster than a retail store. They also come with many different titles. In our travels, we looked for them so we could find good prices. Several items of stationery are sold at these stores, and the price is always right. There are also a variety of food items available at these places, and we took advantage of getting a supply when we were near one.

Interesting things can happen in any store. At a store in California I thought I heard someone speaking Portuguese. This was what we spoke in Brazil. I came around the corner and found a couple with their small daughter. I immediately started speaking Portuguese. They were so surprised that I could speak their language. It was a joy to converse for a few minutes with them. This has happened several times through the years.

Invariably, they all want to know how I could speak their language. This gives a marvelous opportunity to tell them we learned it in Brazil, where we were years ago to tell people about Jesus Christ. We thank God for the witnessing tool

He gave us so we could be testimonies for Him no matter where we are.

Because we shop in Bellingham, Washington, near our home in Ferndale, Washington, many times Canadians shop in the U.S.A. for better prices. The border between the United States and Canada is only 15 miles from where we live. One day I encountered a young couple in Walmart. We chatted in Portuguese, and it was delightful to converse with them in their language. God is so good in opening many ways in which we can share the gospel and tell people about Jesus. Remember Jesus commanded us: ***"Go into all the world and preach the gospel to every creature."*** (Mark 16:15) Are you telling those around you about Him?

GETTING THE MOST OUT OF A SWAMP COOLER

W hen traveling for Shepherds, some states where we ministered were very hot. We remember once pulling into Brawley, California, and the temperature gauge read 118 degrees F. That was hot! Because Margie and air conditioners are not compatible, we chose long ago to use evaporation coolers. In some parts of the country, they are call them swamp coolers.

These coolers use a simple process of water going through shredded wood. Another name for this wood is excelsior. Excelsior is basically a packing material from wood shavings. Companies have developed a very high grade, which is used for cooling purposes. The theory is that warm air drawn through this dampened excelsior by a fan will cool the ambient temperature as much as 10-12 degrees. This is significant in warmer climates. Supposedly, these coolers do not work in climates that are more humid. However, I have built and used them in Brazil to great advantage, so I am convinced they do work even in humid situations.

Maintenance on these machines is necessary. In our travels for Shepherds, periodically I washed the padding to eliminate any musty or mildew odor that was developing. I also cleaned the reservoir, which invariably collected impurities that settled in it. One of the frustrating parts of these coolers was the water pump. They were simply made and not for heavy use. They would get noisy and many times just stop pumping water, and then the cooler no longer worked properly. When we were in Southern California, I had a brainstorm. I went to a landscape nursery store and bought a pump used in garden fountains. I thought I could configure it to work in our cooler, and it turned out to be very good; we have been using it since then. It really solved the problem of getting water to the excelsior pads. We still use these coolers in our home today. The other night when it was 78 degrees in the family room, our bedroom thermometer registered 68 degrees, thanks to our evaporation cooler.

Water, what a precious thing it is! I pray we may desire the Lord as much as we enjoy refreshing water when thirsty. ***As the deer pants for the water brooks, So pants my soul for You, O God.*** (Psalm 42:1)

GETTING NEAR THE END

While in Montana representing Shepherds, we scheduled meetings for 2010 in California. The calendar filled in nicely, and all systems were in place. THEN, I realized that Margie had serious health issues, which intensified. We prayed much about this and decided we should terminate our ministry with Shepherds.

I wrote a personal letter to Dr. Amstutz explaining our situation and expressing our sadness in severing our relationship with Shepherds. It was a very difficult letter to send, because we greatly admired Shepherds and enjoyed representing them so much.

The next morning we received communications from Dr. Amstutz and Dan DiDonato explaining that they wanted us to continue working for Shepherds. This came as a complete surprise, as we were unable to travel anymore. They asked me to cancel our 2010 California meetings and stay home and take care of Margie. At home, we could write letters thanking the churches for their support and prayer help. They wanted me to do this for a year. We were overwhelmed, as we had never encountered an employer more kind and considerate than this.

OUR HOUSE IN FERNDALE

The next year was exciting. I spent my days on the telephone talking to church secretaries and pastors. I wrote letters by the dozens and sent e-mail and texts to scores of individuals and churches. All the time we were doing this, we could visualize the churches with whom we were communicating. Nostalgia filled our hearts as we thought about the wonderful times previously experienced in those churches.

Now this phase of our lives was ending. We never dreamed of having such a special ministry. God providentially gave us this privilege, and we will always be grateful. To be associated with the Home where our daughter Joy lived for more than forty-five years was incredible. We thank Dr. Amstutz, Dan DiDonato, and the Shepherds Board for the great privilege of representing them on the West Coast. To paraphrase Paul's words, ***We thank our God upon every remembrance of you.*** (Philippians 1:3)

WAVES OF NOSTALGIA

$$\textemdash\textemdash\diamond\textemdash\textemdash$$

As we approach the end our Shepherds book, we invariably look back. What we see is an old couple, us, and the extraordinary privilege we had to travel those years for Shepherds. We never dreamed we would have such an opportunity to share our personal story of our daughter Joy, and the unbelievable kindness of Shepherds in housing and caring for her those forty-five plus years. Every time we think of it, gratitude fills our hearts. Telling this story to churches all over the western United States and Alaska was an experience we will never forget. To encourage churches and individuals to pray and support this worthy organization was a thrill. We have often thought how nice it would be if we had younger bodies and could do it all over again.

Our dear Joy is in Heaven, and a rose purchased in Lynden, Washington, the day she died, is a constant reminder of her and Shepherds. We call the rose bush, Joy Bells, my nickname for her. Its botanical name is "The Pink Knock Out Rose," Margie's favorite color. The day of Joy's memorial service, the bush had a single bud. The entire small plant was one of several floral displays on the platform at First Baptist Church, Ferndale, Washington, on the day of her memorial service.

We are encouraged greatly as we receive regular communication from Shepherds. It is such a thrill to read about the Shepherds College. Thank God for Dr. Amstutz and his associates for giving birth to this new concept, and the fabulous results, which are evident by the success stories we hear. What a marvelous present and future ministry God has enabled that branch of Shepherds to witness.

One by one, we hear of clients we have known through the years, who have died. We have fond memories of how they contributed to our lives just by being friends. What a day of rejoicing it will be in Heaven to fellowship again with them and countless others!

Each time we see a fifth wheel trailer, immediate flashbacks come into our minds. I see a driver backing one into its place, and I think of the challenging times I had with that exercise. On the other hand, what excitement we had in parking at so many church lots, and benefitting from fellowship with the pastors and members of the churches. In addition, we had the fantastic opportunity to share Shepherds with thousands.

We are so glad for memories. How special they are! As we grow older, it is sometimes easier to remember what happened long ago. The Bible even speaks of this, and we relate to it. *I remember the days of old; I meditate on all Your works; I muse on the work of Your hands.* (Psalms 143:5)H

Ralph & Margie (07-16-30 to 10-19-2018) Poulson

CONTACTS

SHEPHERDS HOME
1805 15th Avenue, Union Grove, WI 53182-1597
Ph: 262.878.5620
www.shepherdsministries.org

RALPH POULSON
6079 Summit View Pl, Ferndale, WA 98248
PH: 360.384.0937
CELL: 360-599-0936
rpoulson@Juno.com

For the Poulsons' experiences in Brazil,
see Ralph's 2013 book, From a Canoe to a Chevy.